MW00785133

GUNSMITHING
SHOTGUNS

Other Books by
Dave Henderson

The Ultimate Guide to Shotgunning
Shotgunning for Deer
White Tales: A Modern Look at Deer Hunting

GUNSMITHING SHOTGUNS

A Basic Guide to Care and Repair

DAVID R. HENDERSON

The Lyons Press
Guilford, Connecticut
An imprint of The Globe Pequot Press

DEDICATION

To Dawn for the joy, love, and pride you give me.

The Lyons Press is an imprint of The Globe Pequot Press.

Printed in the United States of America

10 9 8 7 6 5 4 3 2 1

ISBN 1-59228-091-9

Library of Congress Cataloging-in-Publication Data is available on file.

CONTENTS

INTRODUCTION

Nearly all shooters begin their relationship with the shotgun with little, if any, knowledge of its actual workings. We know how to load it, work the safety, and trip the trigger, but all other functions are performed by a mysterious internal apparatus that has more moving parts than Janet Jackson.

We trust the invisible mechanics and don't give them much thought as long as the gun works properly. Only a small minority has the curiosity—or, frankly, the need—to further explore how and why their guns work the way they do.

But if you are reading this, you are probably a part of that minority. I'll bet that if you've owned many guns in your life, you probably had an ugly one that you wanted to dress up a little—and probably one or two handsome ones with which you couldn't hit anything. And we've all had shotguns with annoying characteristics that we'd like to fix. What separates the rest of us from the majority is that we have an urge to tinker with our guns rather than dump them or ship them off for someone else to repair.

After all, there must be a way to tame the gun that slaps the heck out of you each time you pull the trigger. Or perhaps you want to tighten your patterns or shift point of impact. Maybe you're just tired of the time and expense involved in taking your gun to a shop for minor repairs.

You will notice that a good portion of this book is dedicated to shotgun hardware, the specific uses of shotguns, and the dynamics of shotgunning. To diagnose or correct a problem, you first need a thorough understanding of shotguns and their various components and functions.

So this book aims to expand your knowledge of shotguns and shotgunning while you learn all the major facets of actual gunsmithing. It's designed to give you the confidence and skill to work on your own guns without a trip to a gunsmithing school. To advance as an amateur gunsmith, you may have to learn to solder, braze, rasp, hone, shape, blue, checker, and finish. And when you actually apply some of what you've learned, you will probably also know your limitations.

While more complex aspects of gunsmithing—such as welding, machining, blueing, parkerizing, case hardening, checkering or metal tempering, plating or coating—are discussed here, you are better off studying them individually with a professional gunsmith, or farming out the work until your skills progress that far.

If you want to advance past the hobby stage in gunsmithing, you'll need a great deal of varied technical knowledge—and a Federal Firearms License. The FFL application process, in this day and age, is about as comfortable and uncomplicated as do-it-yourself root canal. Most of the information provided here is for shooters who wish to work on their own guns and possibly a few others without quitting their day jobs. But if it inspires you to make a career in gunsmithing, so much the better.

Whether you hunt upland birds, waterfowl, turkeys, or deer or get your satisfaction at the patterning board or from busting clay birds, you will find that competently working on your own guns adds another intriguing dimension to shotgunning.

It's important to note up front that I'm not a professional gunsmith. But I have a long and varied background in shotgunning, from shooting clay birds to hunting everything from grouse, ducks, and squirrels to bears, pronghorns, whitetails, caribou, and even bison. And I've written two previous books on the subject.

The late Don Zutz, a world-class human being and one of the most knowledgeable shotgun minds I've ever encountered, once told me that if I ever got to the point where I thought I knew enough about shotguns, I should try my hand at fixing them. Don was right—just as he always was.

Researching *Gunsmithing Shotguns*—basically pestering world-class gunsmiths, many of whom are friends—taught me, as Zutz suggested, just how little I really knew about the hardware and internal workings of scatterguns. So this book represents the culmination of a personal step into heretofore uncharted waters, with a deep bow to guys like master gunbuilder Mark Bansner, gunsmith and stockmaker Rick Hammond, Ithaca Gun expert Les Hovencamp, Frank Brownell and Larry Weeks of Brownells, steel-shot expert Tom Roster, Jess Briley and Chuck Webb of Briley Chokes, Joe Morales of Rhino Choke Tubes, shooting instructor Steve Schultz, Tar-Hunt's Randy Fritz, and, of course, shotgunning author and expert Don Zutz.

I hope it leads you to a higher level of satisfaction with your own shotguns and shooting.

GETTING STARTED

How does one get started in gunsmithing? Well, you obviously have to have the interest and/or maybe the need. After all, more than one smith got started because he simply couldn't justify the time and expense of sending his gun to a gunsmith for a minor repair.

Before you tackle gunsmithing, I'd suggest that you learn as much about shotguns and shotgunning as possible. You must have solid experience with shotguns and their functions before you can begin to understand what makes them fail and how to correct it.

Frankly, the best way to learn gunsmithing is through personal guidance. The days of apprenticing in a gun shop are largely gone in the United States, but the National Rifle Association (NRA) and a variety of specialty gun shops currently offer courses in many aspects of gunsmithing. But you should still have at least a basic background in gunsmithing before attending one of those courses.

There are also several top-flight gunsmithing schools in the country for anyone truly interested in pursuing this field as a career. The training is excellent, but a school is a substantial investment in time and money. There are many gunsmithing-school

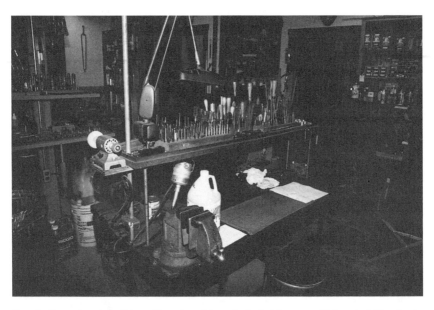

You don't need a shop this well equipped to get started in gunsmithing, but it's nice to have the right tools available when you need them.

A basic shotgun gunsmithing kit.

graduates now working in other jobs simply because they live in an area where there isn't a sufficient customer base to warrant full-time work. Or maybe they were poor businessmen or didn't remain dedicated to their work.

A great alternative to jumping in with both feet—and one taken by most hobbyists delving into the world of gunsmithing—is a home-study course. The advantage is that you learn at your own pace; do the lessons when you want to and turn the work in on your own schedule. There are several good correspondence school courses available, and you can't open a hunting or shooting magazine without finding their ads. The American Gunsmithing Institute (AGI) even offers video courses.

Between correspondence and video courses, I'd definitely recommend AGI. The correspondence schools that I've encountered are often slow to update course material and contact is usually via mail or, in the event of a real problem, over the telephone.

The machine area in this professional shop is clean and organized.

Having a procedure explained on the phone—even by the most knowledgeable, well-meaning instructor—is a poor substitute for actually seeing how it's done.

I encountered one of the big problems with correspondence schools when I started a learn-at-your-own-pace course. After progressing about a third of the way through, I put it on the back burner while I concentrated on a career change. The school demanded that the tuition installments continue, while assuring me that I could "take twenty years to finish if I wanted to."

Well, it was a long lag—about eight years—but when I went back to resume the course, the school wasn't there. That is, there was a gunsmithing correspondence school at that address and using the same telephone number as the one I enrolled in, but it was a different school.

When I explained my situation, I was told that the previous school had sold out to this one and that my old course had been replaced with a new one. Since I'd already paid in full, I assumed that surely there was a way to slip into the current course in some manner. I even offered to pay the difference in

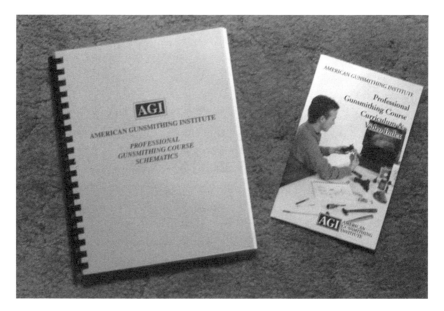

The American Gunsmithing Institute video series allows you to learn at your own pace.

tuition. No dice. Somehow there was a hole in the enrollment records, and they'd never heard of me. Of course, if I wanted to re-enroll with the new school—at full price—they would be glad to accommodate me.

AGI, on the other hand, offers a comprehensive video-training course with simple, clear instruction in everything from the basics of choosing tools and setting up shop to specific training on long guns and pistols and very specific training focused on individual models of guns. Whenever I had a question it was answered quickly and courteously. In many cases, the instructor was able to cite a specific spot in the video from which I was working to illustrate his answer.

Today I have a library of videos for the shotgun models I work on most—Ithaca M37, Remington 870, Remington 1100,

Browning BPS and Auto-5—as well as tapes for my favorite rifles and pistols.

I don't hesitate to work on a gun I'm unfamiliar with. I simply buy the video for that gun and apply the skills I gained from the course. (Contact information for the American Gunsmithing Institute is included in the appendix.)

GUNSMITHING SAFETY

The first rule of gunsmithing safety is to make sure the firearm you are handling is not loaded. The second rule is to treat that gun as if it were loaded at all times anyway.

This may sound overly cautious, even condescending, but little lapses when handling firearms can have grave consequences. It's not the gun that's dangerous, it's how that gun is handled.

A loaded gun laying on a bench is only a harmless paperweight. But that changes quickly when someone picks it up.

Far too many people have handed me guns, assuring me they were empty, only to be embarrassed when I shucked a loaded round on the floor or counter as I checked it automatically. And I've scared myself more than a few times, too.

A wall-mounted fire extinguisher is mandatory in every shop.

There's no such thing as being overcautious.

In addition to the ironclad rules above, there are a few other guidelines to follow at all times when handling firearms.

- Be very careful with trigger pull. Don't work on a trigger unless you are experienced with that particular model—and even then hone it with extreme care. A little too much can be way too much to the operator and may compromise the function and safety of the firearm. Any trigger alteration also voids the gun's warranty.
- Never heat any part of a gun unless you know exactly what you're doing, and always proceed with extreme care.
- Never take excessive amounts of metal from an action at points of stress.
- Never eat or drink from an open cup in your shop, and always clean your hands when leaving the shop. Lead and other toxic elements are likely to be in the air of a gun shop at any time, and you don't want to ingest them.
- Make sure that any replacement parts you install function properly before you attempt to fire the gun.
- Always function-test (and fire) a firearm after repairing it and before returning it to its owner.
- Wear safety goggles when filing, stoning, grinding, cutting, sanding, or working with caustic solutions.
- Never undertake a gunsmithing procedure unless you understand it perfectly. If you aren't sure, seek help.

FINDING WHAT YOU NEED

If you run across a gunsmithing task that seems difficult, if not impossible, to accomplish with normal tools—such as pulling forearms off pump shotguns, disengaging stocks, installing springs in

The Brownells catalog carries virtually every tool or part a gunsmith needs.

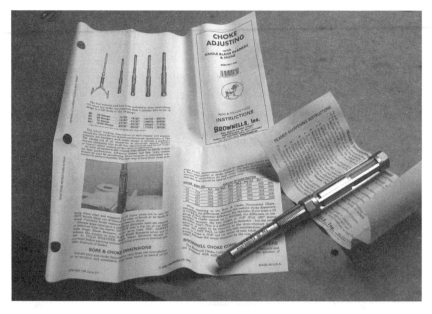

Tools like this reamer come with complete instructions.

certain areas, and so on—rest assured that someone has probably already designed a specialty tool for the job.

It used to be that gunsmithing shops literally made their own specialty tools. But the advent of the pump and the semiautomatic shotgun sparked an increase in firearms production, and as more and more gun manufacturers put out more and more models, the list of specialty tools skyrocketed accordingly.

Many gunsmithing shops stopped smithing and began specializing in tool-making, and they formed the basis for many of today's top tool manufacturers.

That's why the late Bob Brownell, an Iowa gunsmith and toolmaker, decided to start a catalog with products from a variety of companies. The fifty-sixth annual edition of the Brownells catalog was printed by Bob's son Frank in the summer of 2003, with nearly 450 pages listing more than 29,000 tools, parts, books, videos, and sundry products—as well as advice.

It's no exaggeration to say that you'll likely find any tool or part you need in Brownells, the primary purveyor of anything even remotely associated with guns and gunsmithing. I suppose you could compile every catalog from every manufacturer of gunsmithing equipment and check through each until you find what you need, but most of us don't even know many of the small companies who may not advertise or offer regular catalogs.

Brownells offers a fully illustrated assortment of tools and parts, grouped by their use or firearm type. It also offers factory parts made by manufacturers. If you've ever contacted a firearms manufacturer directly about getting a part, you've undoubtedly been floored that the price was not dictated by the part itself but rather by handling and shipping costs and a minimum order limit. It often costs the same to order one hammer spring, action screw, or magazine shell stop from a firearms manufacturer as it would to purchase twenty of them. But you can buy them one at a time through Brownells or the gun parts division of Numrich Arms.

Each tool offered by Brownells comes with clear and thorough (and often illustrated) instructions actually written by someone who has a background in gunsmithing.

I don't even hesitate to tackle a new project these days, as I know that the tool for the job and comprehensive instructions on how to use it are available through Brownells. And if I have a question in virtually any area of gunsmithing—what tool to use, how to use it, or how to accomplish a particular task—I just call their tech-services department toll-free.

Their customer service staff includes a crew of bench-trained, professional gunsmiths. I can tell you from experience that someone on the Brownells staff will know how to solve your gunsmithing problem.

Gunsmith Kinks *is a compilation of techniques and advice that Brownells has assembled for gunsmiths of all levels.*

Midway Supply markets some gunsmithing products not available elsewhere.

The Brownells catalog is available to any firearms aficionado for five dollars, which is refundable with the first order. If you run a shop or business you are entitled to the dealer's discount, which is coded into the item description. Shipping is always $7.50 ($3.60 for tiny items), regardless of weight, the number of boxes, or destination, with no extra handling charges.

If you're looking specifically for gun parts and accessories, check out Numrich Arms in West Hurley, New York. They're the single largest outlet in the country.

Midway Shooting Supplies, which has been a solid resource for shooters, reloaders, and hunters for years, now devotes more than fifty pages of its Master Catalog to gunsmithing.

Since Midway is part of the Battenfeld Group, which includes Frankford Arsenal, Adams & Bennett, Miles Gilbert, Fajen Stocks, and a few other companies, its gunsmithing section lists a few products from these companies that Brownells will not. (Full contact information for the suppliers mentioned above can be found in the appendix.)

Chapter 1

SETTING UP SHOP

The foundation of any gun shop is a functional, efficient work surface. And it should be a dedicated, personal work surface. If you advance past the hobbyist stage, the kitchen table will no longer be sufficient for your gunsmithing activity. Besides, solvents, carbon residue, and general gun gunk are poor spices for your everyday table fare. If you're married, you've undoubtedly already been banished from the kitchen/workshop.

Regardless of your gunsmithing ability, there will be times when an apron spread on your lap will have to suffice as a workbench. But most of the time the bench in your shop is, essentially, your shop. It's the hub of all your work. And for gunsmithing it must be very solid, as it's going to take a lot of abuse. A wobbly bench is, at best, frustrating, and it's simply not functional if you have to chase it all over the room.

I'd also recommend that you steer clear of the pre-assembled cabinet benches available at lumberyards and home-improvement stores. They are usually only two feet deep and four to six feet long, and they're very difficult to make solid. A functional workbench must be of sufficient size and dimension to allow working on elongated objects, and it must be well lit. As you will likely be standing at the bench most of the time, the surface must

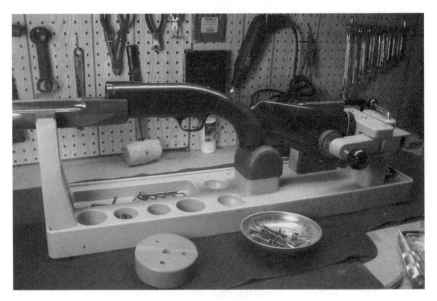

This Tipton gun vise is a fixture on the author's workbench. The magnetic bowl in front of the vise keeps small screws handy.

be at a comfortable height for you or the whole system just isn't going to work.

Your shop isn't your place of business—at least not yet—it's where you go to *escape* your business. Your time there is limited and treasured so the space must be efficient. You don't want to waste all your time rooting through piles of clutter trying to find what you need. Organized, efficient use of space brings peace of mind.

The working surfaces of benches from catalogs are typically thirty-two inches high, which apparently fits some folks. But if you are short, say five-seven or so, that's too high, quickly leading to fatigue in your arms and shoulders if you work for any length of time. A lower surface would be more comfortable. On the other hand, I'm over six feet tall and relatively short-waisted. Working at a bench of standard height for even a short period of time means an aching back.

That's why I built the workbench in my gun shop forty inches high. Through experience I know that's the level at which I can work most comfortably.

A heavy, thick top will stand up to pounding and the occasional torquing required in gunsmithing. A surface that's three or four inches thick works just fine. In fact, a surface made of two-by-fours bolted or doweled face-to-face and sanded flat makes an inexpensive, solid, and durable bench top.

The surface should be smooth to make it easier to wipe up spilled liquids, shot, and powder, but you may want to skip the varnish or polyurethane, as these don't always suffer spilled solvent very well. I topped my bench with a smooth-faced ¾-inch sealed underlayment over two sheets of ¾-inch plywood. You might want to try a smooth wallboard or Formica countertop glued to underlayment or thick plywood.

Brownells offers thick rubber pads that protect the surface from pounding and dampen vibration, and woven fiber mats from Brownells, Cabela's, Remington, Outers, or a variety of other outlets can be used to protect the surface from spills and to catch small screws that would otherwise bounce and/or roll off the smooth, hard surface. Sections of short-nap area

Gunsmith Rick Hammond's shop optimizes available space.

Professional assembly/disassembly mat.

rugs also make good bench coverings for the same reason. Trust me, it's a huge help—tiny screws that leave the bench's surface always seem to vanish into thin air.

And don't skimp on working surface to save space. Again, the bench *is* the workshop. My shop is very small, just less than two hundred square feet partitioned off in one corner of the cellar. Yet I have two benches with a combined surface area of thirty square feet, with plenty of storage space available underneath.

One of the benches is used almost exclusively for gun cleaning, so it's covered with mats and not as strong as the other bench. Cleaning solvents, aerosols, degreasers, lubricants, and other equipment are kept on shelves above the bench within easy reach, and cleaning rods, brushes, patches, jigs, and other specialty cleaning tools are hung out of the way or stored on or under the bench.

An MTM Caseguard cleaning cradle (Portable Maintenance Center) is always on top, and I keep a stainless-steel, lidded barrel pan filled with bore solvent on a shelf beneath it, usually with a couple of barrels soaking.

The other bench is built heavily enough for scope mounting and general gun work. The pegboard wall behind it allows me to hang often-used tools within easy reach, and nearby shelves hold books, measuring devices, marking tools, coffee cups, punches, and everything else I want close at hand but off the work surface. Compartmentalized storage cabinets are also handy for storing hones, extra action screws, choke tubes, and wrenches.

To work effectively, you must have the proper tools.

A plastic Tipton gun vise or an older Decker gun vise is a constant fixture on the bench top, as is a carpet-covered, foot-long section of four-by-four block—something you'll find on most gunsmithing benches. This bench block provides a non-marring "pillow" for stocks, receivers, or whatever else is being worked on.

The bench was designed with room enough for a tabletop chest of drawers at one end, where I store scope rings, bases, a boresighter, forend and stock tools, batteries, and a variety of other things that need to be kept organized yet in close proximity.

Like the cleaning bench, it's well lit by an overhanging fluorescent light and has its own multi-outlet powerstrip. You'll probably find secondary lighting—maybe a goose-necked reading lamp—handy for lighting in situations where you have to

Pegboard provides a wealth of storage options.

look into the myriad dark nooks or crannies of a misbehaving shotgun.

This bench is also drilled to accept my RCBS Grand progressive shotshell reloader, which gets a very heavy workout at certain times of the year but doesn't require a permanent mounting. I can store it under the bench when not in use. With such a cozy shop, I can't afford a bulky drill-press stand or permanently mounted grinder, so I have bench-mount models that also get stored underneath the bench when not in use.

Virtually every square inch of exposed wall in my shop is covered with pegboard to take total advantage of storage space. Paint the pegboard white, along with any other walls and the ceiling,

My RCBS Grand progressive shotshell reloader can be temporarily mounted on the workbench during times of heavy use.

if possible, to get optimum reflection and brightness from your lighting.

Ideally, the floor of your shop should be a surface that is easy to sweep, but there's a downside to this. If it's smooth and easy to clean, anything you drop will likely bounce and roll. And standing on such a surface for long periods of time may not be comfortable. The floor in my shop is concrete, and I cover it with outdoor patio carpeting, which gives a little softer footing and corrals fallen screws and wayward small parts so that they can be retrieved with a magnet. Another advantage is that it can be cleaned with a Shop-Vac. A good alternative would be the rubber mats often used in machine shops and factories.

I have floor-to-ceiling shelving units mounted flush to the wall for storing larger items, such as boxes, cases, and cans. There is also a vertical rack in one corner of the shop for storing guns that I'm working on or that need cleaning. If your shop isn't secure, and you're concerned about who handles the guns, such a rack can be anchored with a cable and lock or you can use specially built locking racks.

A wall-mounted rack keeps cleaning rods close but out of the way.

An open gun rack may not be suitable in a shop that sees a lot of traffic.

My shop has a heavy deadbolt door that's always locked and no windows, so I'm not overly concerned with anyone gaining access when I'm not there. This allows me to use two steel locking gun cabinets instead of an expensive vault. The twin eight-gun cabinets are bolted to the floor and back wall, and the keys are kept in a place that only I know about. Be advised, however, that this situation may not be adequate to satisfy insurance requirements for a professional shop with heavy traffic in guns from paying customers.

Both of my cabinets have silicon moisture-absorbing units that I change regularly, and the shop has a dehumidifier that runs whenever needed.

I store only my personal guns in the shop, and none are truly valuable. My favorites, and anyone else's gun that I happen to have at the time, are in a fourteen-gun Sentry vault with five-bolt lockup and a dial combination in my office/gun room upstairs. It's less than four hundred pounds, fire resistant, and secure against anything short of a torch-wielding thief with sufficient desire and work time.

You can spend a few thousand dollars on a fireproof vault and build your house around it, but I don't think it's really necessary unless your peace of mind or insurance agent demands it. I've seen houses burned to the ground with safes like my Sentry standing in the rubble, with the guns inside only slightly steamed.

Sufficient ventilation is an absolute necessity in your shop. You'll be dealing with fumes from solvents, wood and rubber dust, and other foreign agents that must be vented and/or diluted with fresh air.

As noted, my shop is a partitioned corner of the cellar in our house. The concrete block foundation forms two of the walls, and the other two are studded partition covered with ⅜-inch gypsum board on the outside and old fireproof wallboard on the inside, most of which is covered by pegboard. Any fire that breaks out in the shop will be contained there, and a fire elsewhere in the house won't affect the shop unless the entire structure is destroyed.

It should go without saying that a fire extinguisher and first-aid kit are required items in any shop.

Being a devotee of video instruction, I have a combination television-VCR in one corner of my shop with a shelf of AGI videos within easy reach. Another atypical gunsmithing item found in my shop is a laptop computer. An adequate model can be had for less than a couple hundred dollars at a New-To-U computer mart. It puts gun cataloguing, ballistics programs, book-keeping, even the power of the Internet (if the shop has a tele-phone line) at your fingertips, and doesn't take up any more room than a copy of *Shooter's Bible*.

Computers can be found in most modern gunsmithing shops.

BE CAREFUL, BE CLEAN

"L-e-a-d" is a four-letter word in today's environmentally sensitive (well, environmentally aware) world. While lead is the magic element in ballistics, it can be deadly in more ways than one.

Lead poisoning can be dangerous and debilitating. People who are extremely sensitive to lead should wear a dust mask and rubber gloves when cleaning or working on a firearm.

Gunsmiths should always wash their hands thoroughly with soap and warm water after working with firearms. The bolt and receiver area are typically loaded with very fine lead particles that can get into your lungs and stomach if you eat soon after handling a gun without washing the residue from your hands.

People who shoot at indoor ranges should also be extremely careful. Lead is present in vapor form after each discharge. It is also present in most priming mixtures and in particle form as it shears off from pressure on the driving sides of the rifling lands.

Chapter 2

GUNSMITHING TOOLS

BENCH TOOLS

If the bench is the very foundation of your shop, then a good vise is the most important addition. A bench-mounted vise is your extra hand, your solid grip, and your holder, even a "persuader" when something needs a little more *oomph*.

Don't cut corners when selecting a vise. Get a big, sturdy one. If you get a small hobby vise to save space and money you may find that it isn't sufficiently rugged to hold barrels while you torque out a stubborn choke tube or a receiver in which a barrel is stuck.

Keep in mind, though, that the coarse, serrated gripping surfaces of a rugged bench vise are a poor match for barrels, stocks, or receivers you don't want marred. Brownells and other gunsmith supply houses have leather, brass, lead, and aluminum/polymer-faced liners that grip securely but won't mar finishes.

Although barrel presses—used to grip a barrel so that it can be torqued off a receiver—are a staple in riflesmithing shops, a shotgun gunsmith will seldom find a need for one. There are times, however, when you may need to remove a barrel from a bolt-action or solid-frame gun (like the Ithaca DeerSlayer II or

A bench vise must have leather, lead, aluminum, or plastic grip inserts to avoid marring the wood or metal being worked on.

High Standard Flite King). For shotgunners, it's probably easier to farm out this work since a barrel press often requires a more solid foundation than the average bench can provide.

Since I also work on rifles, I did invest in a barrel press. It's mounted on a four-hundred-pound, steel-topped table with eight-inch-square legs that I rescued from the press plate–making room of an ancient newspaper building where I was once employed. It also serves as an alternate stand for my drill press or shotshell reloading press.

Gunsmith Rick Hammond, who you'll see featured in several photos in this book, has his barrel press mounted on a fifty-five-gallon diesel drum filled with rocks and concrete. He estimates that it weighs twelve hundred pounds, and it never wanders far from the end of his workbench.

One tool you will definitely need is a drill press, whether it's a stand-alone or a bench-top model like mine. Make sure it has at least thirteen or fourteen inches of clearance between the chuck and the plate; working on a shotgun eats up more space than you might expect. A couple of power hand drills can handle other jobs.

A bench-top grinder is really handy for sharpening, grinding blades, and so on, but it's really messy (throws ground-off debris

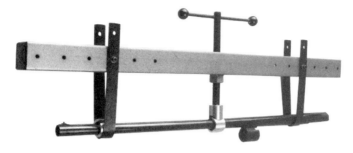

A barrel press manufactured by B-Square.

everywhere) for other work. You may want to use it in an area away from your shop.

It's essential to have some sort of motorized rotary tool like a Dremel, Foredom, or my Bench Weasel. In fact, these can usually be substituted for a grinder or polishing wheel without much loss of function in many cases.

A handheld belt sander is perfectly adequate for my woodworking needs. In fact, due to its mobility, I prefer it to bench models for stock work and fitting recoil pads.

A large professional or specialty shop may also have lathes, cutters, milling machines—maybe even welding equipment, a parts

Every gunsmith needs a good drill press, whether a stand-alone machine like this or a smaller bench-top model.

Mount your bench grinder in an area that is easy to clean up, as it will create a lot of loose debris.

Rotary tools are always useful in a gun shop. The author has a Bench Weasel that hangs out of the way when not in use.

washer, and blueing tanks. But a basic, light-duty gunsmithing shop doesn't need this equipment.

If you have a machine shop and/or fabricating background you may want to do your own metal work, but lathes and milling machines and, to a lesser extent, welding outfits and blueing systems, are major investments and you'll undoubtedly have to wrestle with how you can justify the cost—or find the space.

Most gunsmiths farm this work out. Of course, as your interest in gunsmithing grows, you'll have ample opportunity to add specialized machinery to your shop.

A lot of professional shops have a bullet trap in one corner. A ¾-inch plywood box lined with sheet metal and filled at least eighteen inches deep with sand will suffice as a shot trap for function-testing a shotgun. But it's a very loud process to carry out indoors and largely unnecessary if you live close to a suitable shooting range.

COMMON HAND TOOLS

SCREWDRIVERS

One hand tool you'll use constantly in your shop is the screwdriver. I'm sure you've read this a thousand times before, but it bears repeating: When working on guns, always use the correct size and type of screwdriver for the screw. Screwdriver blades should match the thickness and width of the screw, and they should be hollow ground or parallel ground so they fit snugly and don't slip.

Screwdrivers from the local hardware store have tapered blades to "fit" more screws. But using one of these on a gun will leave you with a distorted slot or marred finish, because the poor-fitting blade usually slips from the slot and makes a free bore "engraving" run.

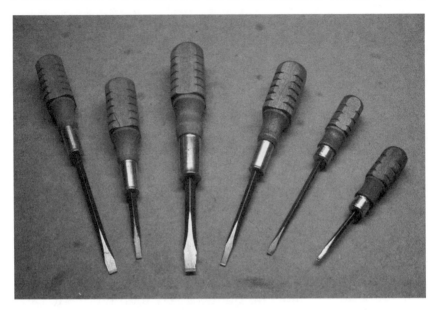

Fixed-blade gunsmithing screwdrivers are designed specifically to fit gun screws.

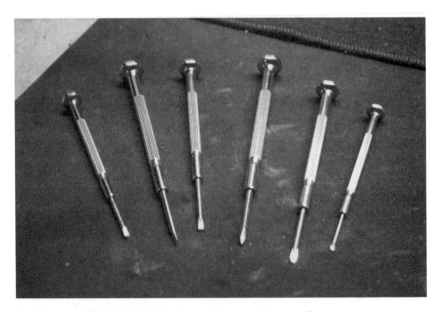

Precision screwdrivers handle jobs that regular screwdrivers can't.

The only situation where a common screwdriver may be of use in a gunsmith shop is in removing the long bolt that secures the buttstock to the receiver. Today, most of these are hex bolts (7/16 inch is common), but a foot-long Sears screwdriver will suffice for any that still have slotted bolts.

If the screw is a Phillips head, the suggestion is the same — make sure your screwdriver is the same size. Virtually all small Phillips heads will fit in all Phillips-head screws, but using the wrong size driver is just asking for problems.

You'll see "gunsmithing" multiple-head screwdriver sets advertised in a lot of catalogs. But be advised that bits in the twenty-dollar kits are commonly too soft for heavy-duty extraction work on stubborn screws.

I'm a gorilla with a screwdriver and have warped a variety of lower-priced "specialty" blades that had to be ground to another shape to regain any usefulness. High-quality gunsmithing screw-

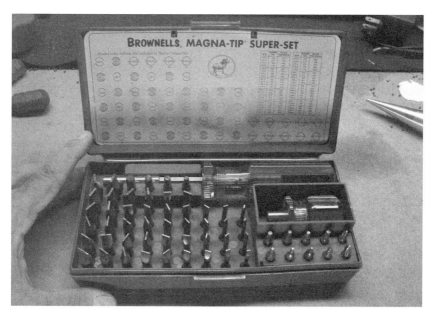

Brownells Magna-Tip Super Set includes just about every driver tip you'll ever need.

drivers are hard, so the blade will break before it deforms under load and jumps the slot. I've also used so-called specialty sets where the blades were simply too brittle.

You can throw away a lot of money, one twenty-dollar bill at a time, searching for suitable screwdrivers, or you can actually save money by spending more and getting a good set.

You can't go wrong with the Magna-Tip Master screwdriver set from Brownells. It is a basic requirement in any shop, as it will have a bit for virtually every screw you encounter and stands up to a good deal of abuse. Fixed-blade gunsmithing sets and torx- or hex-head drivers will be helpful as your skills advance.

If you do much work you will undoubtedly want to grind screwdriver blades to fit specific screws. I have a Browning Auto-5 that was passed down from my dad; I love it dearly but curse it regularly. The screw slots are narrower than any commercial blade I've ever found. The only answer to working on narrow-slotted screws is to simply grind a screwdriver blade to fit and put it away in a labeled drawer where it can be found the next time that specific need arises.

When grinding a screwdriver blade with a bench grinder or rotary tool, use caution not to overheat the tip or you will compromise (soften) the metal. If the tip turns blue, it's overheated. At this point you can reheat it with a propane torch and douse it in oil or grind the shaft back to hard steel and then grind a new tip.

HAMMERS

The next most important hand tools in my shop are hammers. A small ball-peen hammer is considered sufficient in many shops. The normal mindset is that very little pounding is needed in gunsmithing.

But I'm a little less conservative and have a lot more hammers. A large, rubber-headed (rawhide also works well) hammer is great

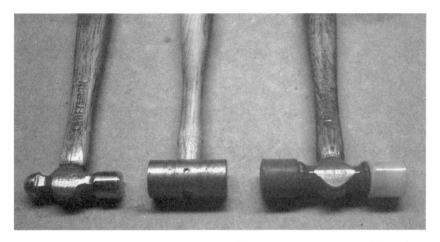

Ball-peen, brass, and plastic-coated hammers all see regular use in a gunsmithing shop.

for soft-face tapping or for persuading stubborn objects without scarring them. And the small ball-peen hammer is handy for peening surfaces to provide a tighter fit or delicately restore the heads of buggered irreplaceable screws. You'll also find brass-headed hammers useful for driving pins flush, and a non-marring plastic-faced hammer is nice to have around. I also have a light tack hammer on the rack that I seem to find a use for virtually every day.

PIN AND DRIFT PUNCHES

All shotguns are held together with screws and/or pins, with many "newer" American designs relying heavily on the latter. Remington 870s, 1100s, and 11–87s, for example, use a screw to hold the stock, but everything else is held together with pins. You'll need a set of drift punches (stronger punches, used with more force) or pin punches to remove or reset those pins.

There is nothing wrong with lubricating a pin to ease its passage into a hole, and it may pay dividends later if that pin needs to be removed. Generally speaking, you should try to match the diameter of the punch with the diameter and shape of the pin's head.

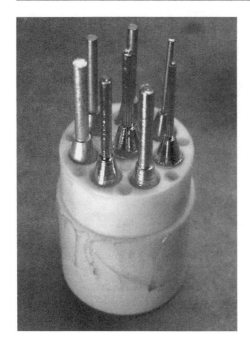

Every shop needs a good set of brass and steel punches and drifts.

Brass pin punches are usually recommended for drifting sights, and some smiths use them on pins and other blued surfaces. But brass pin punches can leave a yellow smear on a blued surface that is very difficult to remove. It's easier to avoid this by using steel punches.

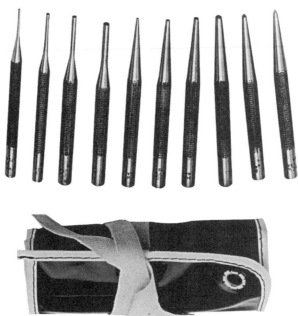

Brownells professional punch set.

There are, surprisingly, a lot of different types of pins in guns, and they all are used a little differently, and driven a little differently.

The simplest, most common pin is, of course, the straight pin (unhardened) or dowel (hardened). They are cylindrical and commonly made of carbon steel. Standard pin and drift punches are adequate for dealing with these, whether they are slave pins (used to drive out another pin and temporarily take its place), slip fit (the pin has a smaller diameter than the hole), or interference fit (the pin has a slightly larger diameter than the hole). The biggest visible difference between the types is that the dowel pins often have chamfered ends that make them easier to start in place.

Spiral pins aren't much different from straight pins, but they hold more securely. These are made of rolled spring steel flat stock and must be compressed by the radius of the hole to fit.

A roll or spring pin looks like a spiral pin split longitudinally and is used to fasten two pieces together that aren't going to be pivoting in relation to each other. They have good holding power, and it takes a bit of elbow grease to drive them out. It's best to use a special roll-pin punch (one end is rounded) on these pins, but you'll only find these through gunsmithing tool outlets. These punches are also useful for driving spiral pins.

Tapered pins are simply straight pins with a smaller diameter on one end. They are driven into specific holes and can only be driven out in one direction. They are always hardened and have domed ends and can be driven with standard pin or drift punches.

Top dead center punch.

Splined or grooved pins are actually dowel pins with chiseled grooves or raised splines on the side, and they're made of unhardened carbon steel. The alterations in the pin surfaces are designed to increase holding power. They are often used as pivot pins and don't take kindly to removal. They should be started with a hammer and set with a drift punch once they are deep enough in the hole.

Ball-end pins are essentially dowels with a rounded end, usually just for aesthetics. They must be driven with a cup-ended punch to avoid flattening the rounded face.

You may run across other types of pins, such as cotter, Clevis, and detent pins, but I've never seen them used in shotguns. Most are designed for use in pistols.

WRENCHES AND PLIERS

Certainly no shop of any kind is complete without a set of wrenches and a set of sockets with a ratchet and/or driver. I have a set of imperial (American) and metric box wrenches hanging from the pegboard over my bench, the sizes nearest in dimension

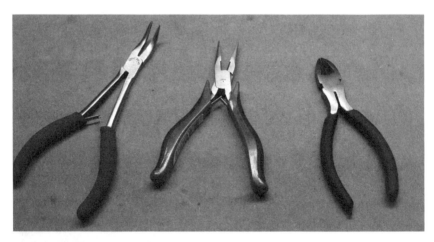

You'll need a variety of pliers for gunsmithing tasks.

each sharing a board pin. The sockets are in an always-open box snug to the back wall of the bench.

Pliers are also a must—at least one pair of needle-nosed, a set with parallel jaws, and maybe one or two curved-nose and cutting types. There is a set of firm-gripping battery pliers in every one of my shops. They are the most useful gripping tool extant—equal to the lever Archimedes boasted he could use to move the world. Well, almost. And a set of Vise-Grips is a handy addition to any shop, as are tweezers.

FILES

Files are another important group of hand tools. My dad was a toolmaker, and part of his apprenticeship was to use a file to turn a steel block into a sphere. Once you know how to use a file correctly and efficiently, you can learn any type of metal work.

Whether on metal or wood, files are used for shaping, smoothing, and making things fit better. They are normally classified according to their shape or cross-section, the pitch or spacing of their teeth, and the nature of the cut.

A file's cross-section may be triangular, quadrangular, circular, or round on one side and flat on the other. The outline of its contour can be tapered from a wide rear to a narrow point or blunt with parallel sides. A file's "cut" refers to the arrangement of its teeth, such as single, double, rasp, or curved.

A single-cut file has one series of parallel teeth across the face, arranged at an angle to the axis of the file. The angle depends largely on the nature of the file's use. Single cuts are typically used with light pressure for finish work.

For rougher work, where more material needs to be removed with each stroke, a double-cut file is better. Double cuts feature small, pointed teeth angled toward the point of the file and arranged in two series of diagonal rows that cross each other.

Brownells file starter set.

A rasp is used on wood and features large, rounded teeth that are applied with heavy pressure to remove copious amounts of material with each stroke.

The curve-toothed file features coarse, single-cut teeth in a set of parallel arcs across the face.

Files can also be broken into five separate classes: Swiss pattern files, mill or saw files, machinist's files, curved-tooth files, and rasps. Swiss pattern files are typically used for delicate work. Their points are smaller, their tapers longer, and they are available in much finer cuts than other types of files.

Mill or saw files, known as American patterns, are commonly used for sharpening blades or rough-working a surface where finish isn't critical. Machinist's files have a variety of uses, depending on the coarseness of their teeth, and curved-tooth or needle files are designed for getting into difficult places, such as checkering cuts.

If you spend any time working with files, you will undoubtedly adopt a favorite shape and use it in different designations of coarseness. I like the feel of a six- or eight-inch Swiss pattern pillar file with a versatile medium-fine cut, maybe a No. 2 or No. 3

Learning to file wood and metal correctly will serve you well.

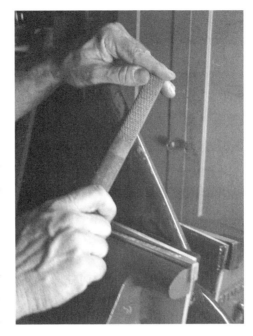

coarseness. Depending on the size of your hands, the type of work you're doing, and maybe your favorite angle of attack, you may prefer an American pattern or other type of file in a different size.

File strokes are always made in one direction, usually away from your body, often with your off hand guiding the blade's downward pressure and direction. When using a file on metal, small chips can become imbedded in the file's teeth, decreasing its effectiveness. You can use something to remove those chips (a rifle cartridge case with the mouth flattened to a blade works well when run through file grooves), or you can run the file across a bar of file chalk regularly.

When working on a wood stock you'll most often use a round or half-round rasp, working around the curves of the cheekpiece or in the multidirectional curves of the grip area. Always try to keep the file or rasp blade running in the direction of the wood grain. It's easier and requires less finish sanding than working across the grain.

ABRASIVE STONES

Just as filing well requires a bit of practice, so does the use of an abrasive stone on metal. Many gunsmiths never reach a comfortable level with stones.

41

Nevertheless, they are important gunsmithing tools, and you should have a working knowledge of stones if you do much gun work. Abrasive stones, whether synthetic or natural, come in various degrees of coarseness, as defined by the size of the granules in the stone. The shape of the granules is also important in determining the smoothness of the metal finish, and the hardness of the stone determines how easily it will deform.

Some steel can't be cut with files, but a stone will do the job. Likewise, a soft stone will finish steel to a finer surface than any file. Hardness is a matter of chemical makeup and physical structure of the stone, and while the types of stone—Arkansas, Washita, India, polycrystalline ruby, diamond, and the synthetic carborundum or ceramic—all have different qualities and characteristics, their description goes beyond the scope of this book.

If you reach the point in gunsmithing where stones are part of your work, you can easily find a reference to determine which is best for your particular application.

The most commonly used stone in any shop (outside of the stone bits in rotary tools) is a flat, fine stone with a 90-degree edge used to worry sears and sear-notches. Long, thin, hard stones can be used to touch up the inside of a bore at the bottom of newly drilled ported holes. Stones aren't used very often on wood, primarily because they tend to build up heat and burn the wood.

Aluminum, magnesium, lead, tin, and zinc alloys will load up a stone and then scratch steel badly. Magnesium fouling in a stone, such as a grindstone, can flash or explode when steel and iron are touched against it.

Stones must be oiled or washed regularly to float away metal particles that would otherwise compromise cutting ability and eventually scratch surfaces. Washing them in water is easiest because it involves no cleanup, but there are commercial honing oils designed specifically for stone cleaning, and it's impossible to use them too often. I've also heard of gunsmiths using glass cleaner on diamond lapping wheels.

OTHER POLISHING TOOLS

Stones are just one type of abrasive used for hand polishing. Emery cloth or aluminum-oxide cloth is typically used in hand polishing a finish in preparation for blueing, but machine polishing is also possible with wheels covered with hard felt, wire bristles, air bladders, loose muslin, or spiral-sewn muslin.

Hand or machine polishing is accomplished in roughly the same manner—using successively finer grits until the desired polish is achieved. When machine polishing, you must always keep the work moving under the wheel. Regardless of the polishing material, the surface can easily be "scooped" if it stops momentarily.

When polishing flat surfaces, work from the center toward the edge, which will keep the wheel from rounding over the edge. Around screw holes, polish toward the edge and rotate the piece around the hole to prevent dishing it. Always polish so the wheel leaves the work, never so that the edge of the work is introduced to the wheel first.

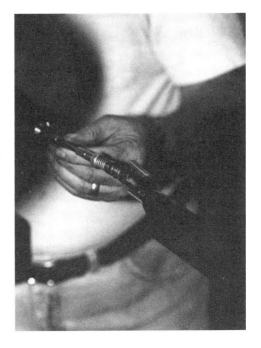

Barrel hones are used to polish the interior of shotgun bores.

TAPPING AND DIE-CUTTING

You may not need them to get started, but if you stay in gunsmithing for any length of time you'll undoubtedly find a need for tap-and-die and drill-and-tap sets.

The reason so many modern guns are fastened together with pins rather than screws is because it requires less time, work, and expense to simply drill a hole and leave it versus drilling it and cutting threads into it.

Although pins are effective and efficient holders, true gun fanciers abhor them, while virtually worshipping the perceived workmanship involved in precision screw holes. There is no question that the screw is one of the most efficient fastening devices ever created. Regardless of pitch or pattern, more than 99 percent of the load against a screw is taken by the first three threads. The other threads only serve to introduce the screw to the hole, and the fifth is always relaxed—an engineering marvel.

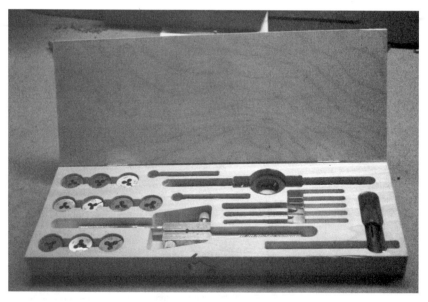

A tap-and-die set belongs in every serious shop.

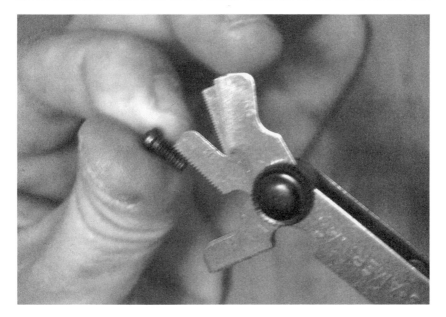

A thread gauge is necessary for drilling and tapping.

Despite the proven efficiency of the "wedged axis," we're going to see far more pins than screws in future firearms. But a modern gunsmith still needs to be acquainted with threads and how screw holes are fashioned.

If you are going to do more than just disassemble and clean your firearms—jobs like mounting accessories and scopes or removing broken screws—you'll find a tap-and-die set virtually essential.

You should know that threads are identified in the American (imperial) system by number sizes and fractions of inches and diameter and thread pitch. Com-

Straight thread pitch gauge.

mon sizes also include a description of whether the thread is standard coarse or fine thread. A gunsmith is always looking for an exact match, which means he better be well-versed in decimals, since the trend is toward translating the old designations such as #8–32 thread to something like .138–32 THD.

There are several ways to put threads on a shaft, although the only method gunsmiths are concerned with is cutting with a tap. Rolling (actually forging the metal using pressure rather than impact) produces the strongest threads, but this process is far beyond the means of the average gunsmith.

Types of Taps

Thread-cutting taps for cutting female threads into a hole are designated as taper, plug, or bottom taps. The taper tap, which is used to cut threads in a hole that goes through a piece (or to start threads in a deep or blind hole), is pointed, and the cutting edges gradually widen the farther they are from the point. This allows the tap to shave metal instead of pushing it out of the way with pressure. It is the easiest tap to use.

Taprite tap guide.

Plug taps require more force due to the fact that they shave metal in larger sections. They are called plugs because they're blunt at one end and have a steeper angle of taper.

Bottom taps are also blunt and are used to cut threads to the bottom of a blind hole or to a certain depth in a deep hole. The most common threads you'll encounter are 4–40, 6–32, 6–48, 8–32, and 10–32, and if you're just getting started in gunsmithing it's probably best to get plug taps in those sizes. It takes a little more work to start plug taps, but they are more versatile than taper or bottom taps. Once you have the basic plug taps and gain some experience with them, you can add other types of taps to your arsenal.

Most screws on sights and scope mounts are 6–48, and many shotgun beads are 8–40. You should drill the pilot hole to start your tap at the minor diameter of the thread. That way you are removing only the metal where the thread grooves will eventually be, instead of setting up a situation where the tap has to enlarge the hole. (They aren't designed to handle this.) Keep a drill-size/tapping-pilot-hole chart handy to eliminate guesswork.

Tapping or cutting oil is essential when cutting threads. There is a wide assortment of oils available, but some don't work with aluminum and only the heavier ones should be used on stainless steel or other hardened steel.

Tap handles are a matter of preference. You'll probably start with a T-handle type and be happy with it unless, by some quirk, you get a chance to use another type that you take a shine to.

Tap guides and tap extensions are accessories that aren't absolutely necessary for most gunsmithing jobs, but they may come in handy in certain applications.

Depending on the type of metal, cutting fluid, and the size of the hole, the tap should be turned about 30 to 45 degrees and reversed about the same amount to clear the threads of cuttings. If they aren't cleared, the cuttings will start doing their own extracurricular tapping, and the threads will be, shall we say, unique. Whether you're cutting male threads with a die or female threads with a tap, interrupting the advancing cut with some short reversals is essential to avoid trouble.

MEASURING INSTRUMENTS

You won't get far into gunsmithing, or any other metal work, before you find a need for precision measuring devices. You'll need metal rules, called gauges, for linear measurements and more precise (and complicated and expensive) devices to take other critical measurements.

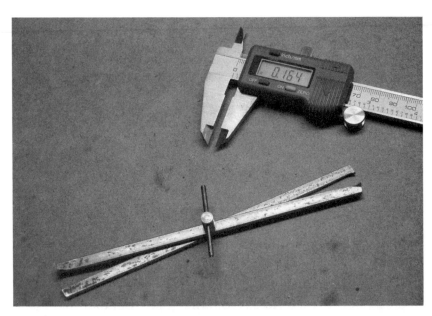

Wing and dial calipers can perform almost any small measurement.

You probably won't be fabricating gun parts or specialty tools early in your gunsmithing career, so your basic measuring needs will be largely confined to determining chamber and forcing-cone lengths, internal choke diameters, and possibly barrel-wall thickness.

These dimensions can be obtained with instruments that fall into two categories: direct and indirect (or comparison) measuring devices. An example of a direct measuring device would be a gauge or rule, a micrometer, or dial-face caliper.

Indirect, or comparison, devices take a measurement—usually in a place or situation where it's impossible to use direct measuring devices—and maintain that dimension so it can then be measured by a direct measuring device. Inside calipers, for example, can be inserted into barrels to take a measurement, then locked and brought out to be measured by a rule or dial caliper.

The dial caliper is the precision measuring device of choice these days, while older machinists like my dad preferred vernier calipers and micrometers. Maybe it's our generation, but today's workers seem to prefer the simple digital or clock-face read afforded by dials as opposed to the intricate finger-tuning, eye-crossing small delineations and mental gymnastics involved in using and interpreting micrometers.

My suggestion would be to get instruments that you are already familiar with and/or can understand, and to get the best quality you can afford. Let your prospective use of the instrument determine the quality you'll need. For instance, only a professional gunsmith with everyday machining and tool- and part-marking capabilities needs a thousand-dollar instrument. Most of us can make do with a decent, quality instrument for a much-reduced price because it won't be used as extensively or regularly.

Regardless of the price, it's wise to keep precision instruments clean and store them correctly, as mistreated tools can give

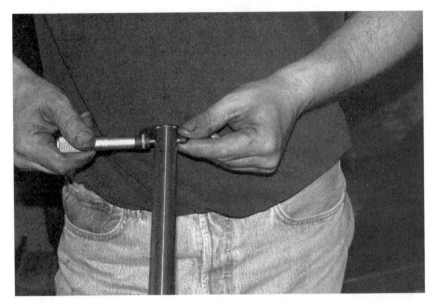

A micrometer caliper is extremely accurate, but it takes a trained hand to interpret its readings.

misleading readings. It's wise to leave a small gap between measuring surfaces when storing calipers and similar devices. This allows the different metals and shapes to expand and contract with temperature changes without stressing against each other and possibly compromising the tool's accuracy.

After all, a measuring device that gives an erroneous reading is worthless, and maybe even dangerous.

Dial Calipers

The dial caliper has four basic uses: direct inside, outside, and depth measurements and measurements of dimensions obtained by indirect measuring devices. They generally measure to the thousandth of an inch or its metric equivalent. That may not be precise enough for machine or lathe work, but it's well within acceptable parameters for the average gunsmith.

Starrett electronic calipers.

With either the digital or dial-face calipers, it's best to clean and close the jaws and adjust the dial bezel to zero before opening the jaws to take a measurement. Apply only enough pressure to the jaws or depth stem to assure that contact has been made. With a little experience you will develop a feel, and light, consistent pressure will become habit.

SPECIALTY TOOLS

There are literally hundreds of specialty tools for gunsmithing, from barrel presses and chamber and forcing-cone reamers to barrel hones, sight-drilling jigs, spanner wrenches, action wrenches, and bolt-removing tools. Many such tools are specialized to the point that they are built for only one model of firearm. The variety you'll see while leafing through a Brownells catalog will leave you astounded.

Most gunsmiths start with the basic tools already discussed, then expand their inventory as the need arises. However, there are a few specialized tools that you can acquire now that will not often lie idle if you go very far in gunsmithing.

One is a screw holder gizzie—a tweezer-like spring steel gripper that's handy for holding small screws while you work on them.

A specialty wrench for gripping magazine caps will see use over and over, and I can't really remember what I did before I got a screw-removal jack. Actually, I do remember, but I try to suppress such dark thoughts to retain my sanity.

Another "what did I ever do before I got this" tool is a bench block. This is basically a machinist's block, a short cylinder made

A screw holder gizzie is useful for working with small screws.

It's helpful to have a spanner wrench when removing the forend on a pump shotgun.

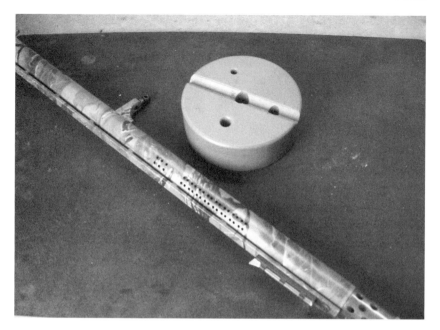

A bench block acts as an extra hand on the work surface.

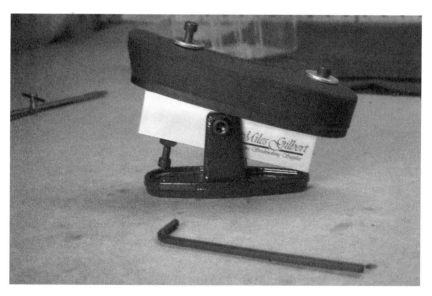

A recoil pad installation jig makes it easier to shape and fit a pad without damaging the gunstock.

of plastic or steel with a V-groove cut across the diameter to hold a barrel, receiver, or other workpiece off the bench surface while you drive out pins or perform other work.

A set of spring-catch hooks will also aid in making seemingly impossible jobs relatively simple.

A trigger gauge is another specialty tool that you'll need early and often. Stock- and forearm-removal tools and a couple of spanner wrenches should also be part of your tool inventory.

A recoil pad installation jig will pay for itself with the first job, as will a stuck-choke-tube-removal wrench.

Chapter 3

ALL ABOUT SHOTGUNS

ORIGIN OF THE SHOTGUN

A shotgun is essentially a firearm that operates under relatively low chamber pressure to throw short-range loads of pellets or single projectiles (slugs).

It's difficult to determine how long shotguns have been around since all early shoulder-fired arms shot single balls or groups of balls. When were they shotguns and when were they muskets? The first cannons, or *gonnes*, were technically shotguns because they were smoothbores loaded with multiple projectiles (basically rocks, nails, or other nasty stuff).

We know there were individually carried firearms in existence in the 1400s, so the origin of the shotgun is largely a matter of semantics or nomenclature. Those fifteenth-century matchlocks evolved into wheel locks, then *snaphaunces* and *miquelets*, and eventually side-by-side English flintlocks in the latter half of the eighteenth century.

Wingshooting became more practical with the introduction of the percussion cap in the early 1800s. The first slide-action (pump) shotguns appeared in the 1880s, and John Browning's lever-action shotgun was produced by Winchester in 1887. The

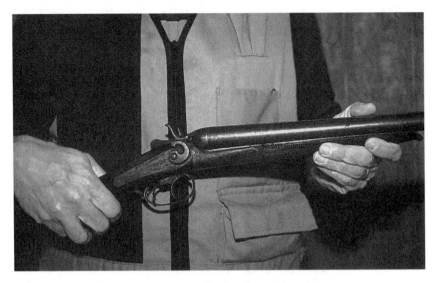

Exposed-hammer shotguns were common in the nineteenth century.

first viable autoloader was Browning's A-5, which was introduced in the early days of the twentieth century.

Today's shotguns are delineated by the gauge system rather than calibers. Historically, the term *gauge* refers to the number of equal-sized balls cast from one pound of lead that would pass through a barrel of specific diameter. The 12-gauge's bore would allow a dozen balls of equal size to pass through, the 20-gauge twenty balls, and so on. The 16-gauge is the classic example since that gauge accommodates sixteen 1-ounce lead balls.

Shotgun manufacturers still refer to gauges in their models, but they use decimal measurements to identify choke constrictions. The system of expressing shotgun bore sizes by gauge rather than by decimal or metric measurements is, like many things related to smoothbores, a matter of tradition. All of the modern gauges are identified by normal measurements, except the runt of the litter, the .410-gauge, which is labeled by its bore diameter. One explanation may be that the English numbered gauge system's smallest gauge was the 50, which measured 0.453 inch. Presumably, anything smaller needed to be labeled by diameter, which saves us from going squirrel hunting with a 67.5-gauge.

At one time, letter gauges were used for some very large bore sizes, with "A" the largest at a two-inch diameter, "B" at 1.938, on down to "P" at 1.250 inches.

The largest gauge common today is the 10. Manufacturers originally chambered this gauge for 2⅞-inch shells, but the current chambers are 3½ inches. Today the 10-gauge is a specialty gun used by goose and turkey hunters and those who chase deer with buckshot. The only guns currently chambered for 10-gauge are the Browning BPS pump, H&R (New England Firearms) single shot, and the Remington SP-10 (successor to the Ithaca Mag-10) and Browning Gold autoloaders.

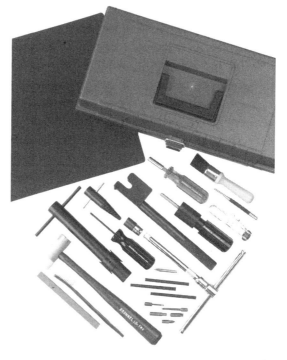

The advent of the 3 ½-inch, 12-gauge put the demand for 10-gauges in decline. The 12 is the world's most popular gauge because it can handle anything from very light to very heavy loads in 2¾-, 3-, and 3½-inch chambers.

A tool layout for Remington's most popular shotguns.

In lighter shotguns, the 20-gauge is a sensible alternative to the heavier, harder-recoiling 12. The in-between 16-gauge was mostly phased out in the 1980s. The 20 is a common choice among upland bird hunters seeking a physically lighter gun to tote on long days afield. It is one of the four gauges in skeet competition, and with its ⅞- and 1-ounce loads, it is effective on small game. There are 3-inch, 20-gauge loads and chambers available, but most aren't conducive to good patterning.

The 28-gauge may be the most useful of the small bores due to its comfortable size and effective ¾-ounce payload, but its use is primarily limited to bird hunting. While it's also a popular skeet gauge, the 28 is often overlooked in favor of the more powerful 20 in the field.

The .410, another skeet gauge, is pretty much limited to shooting small vermin due to its tiny payload, although you'll find exceptions among dedicated upland bird hunters shooting in specific situations and youngsters heading to the squirrel woods.

Actually, the gauge system was continued for rifles in gauges up to No. 1 (1.669 inches) until the middle of the twentieth century and is still correct, although rarely used, for smoothbores intended to shoot a single bullet. The system was abandoned when rifle bullets became increasingly elongated, making bore size a less meaningful indication of the weight of the bullet.

It wasn't until the 1840s that tool-making and gauging techniques were precise enough to measure gun bores with anything like the accuracy that we see today. It was, however, always practical to classify bores by the approximate weight of the ball they took, although this didn't signify a precise specification of bore diameter. The present standard bore diameters, though specified on the old rule, became possible only with the ability to make accurate measurements.

According to the Sporting Arms and Ammunition Manufacturers Institute (SAAMI), the following are nominal bore diameters: 10-gauge, 0.775 inch; 12-gauge, 0.729; 16-gauge, 0.665; 20-gauge, 0.615; 28-gauge, 0.550; and .410-gauge, 0.410. Obsolete gauges that remain in SAAMI specifications include the 4-gauge (1.052 inches), 6-gauge (0.919), and 8-gauge (0.835). I've also seen 24-gauge (0.579), 32-gauge (0.526), and 36-gauge (0.506) guns, which have been relegated to wall-hanger status by the lack of suitable loads.

SHOTGUN ACTIONS

Gunsmiths must deal with five types of actions in modern shotguns: pumps, autoloaders, bolt actions, double barrels, and single shots. Each type comes with advantages and disadvantages.

THE PUMP GUN

The pump is the quintessential American action. It's been around since the 1880s (first designed in 1852) and became extremely popular in the middle of the twentieth century when doubles priced themselves out of the general marketplace and the hunting-gun market exploded in the wake of WWII.

The pump has been the most popular style of repeating shotgun ever since. It features a single barrel over a tubular magazine, and the action operates by pulling the forend rearward on a rail to

The Remington 870 is a classic pump gun.

Magazine tube/cap pliers.

trigger the ejection of the spent hull. Pushing the forend forward feeds a new shell from the magazine to the chamber and locks the breechbolt back to battery, ready for the next shot.

Classic American pumps include the Winchester Model 12 and exposed-hammer Models 1897 and 97, the Ithaca M37 and Browning BPS, and the Remington Models 31 and 870. The latter is still a bestseller, despite the fact that nearly ten million are already in circulation.

The pump action offers simplicity, durability, low price, and a lighter weight, but you will likely pay for those advantages with heavier recoil. The compact, lightweight aspect of the pump makes it the darling of the deer stalker and upland bird hunter, and its quick, simple action attracts waterfowlers who ply their trade in elements that can foul up more sophisticated actions. Follow-up shots are also easier with a pump than with any action other than an autoloader.

Remington 12-, 16-, and 20-gauge 870s and the 12- and 20-gauge Mossberg 500 and 12-gauge 835 Ultri-Mag are among the international sales leaders every year. Ithaca's M37 pump comes in 12-, 16-, and 20-gauge specialty configurations for deer hunters, waterfowlers, turkey hunters, small game and bird hunters, and claybird shooters. These range from a sub-six-pound, 20-gauge featherweight to the eleven-pound, 12-gauge, bull-barreled Deer-Slayer III, which is available only by special order.

Benelli's futuristic Nova, designed out of polymers, with the stock and lower receiver one piece and the barrel and upper

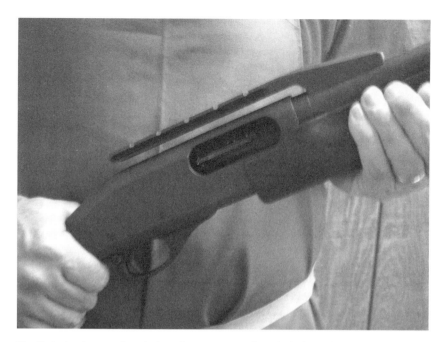

The first step in removing the barrel on a repeater is to lock the action open.

Next, removing the magazine cap frees the barrel on most pump guns.

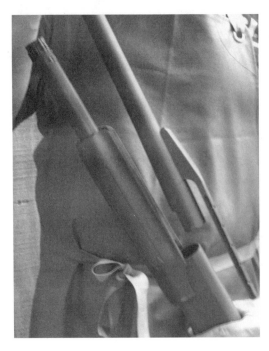

The barrel then slides over the magazine and out of the receiver.

receiver another, is making its presence felt in the marketplace with the American pumps. Charles Daly and several other companies offer pump guns made overseas.

With the exception of the Nova, pumps can be disassembled by removing the recoil pad, and loosening the long stock nut found within, to detach the buttstock from the receiver. The trigger mechanism and other parts of the action are held in

Older versions of the Ithaca Model 37 pump used a magazine cap screw that cammed upward to lock against the barrel lug or downward to release the lug and the barrel.

place with pins or screws, or a combination of both, through the receiver.

With most pumps, the trigger assembly drops out of the bottom of the receiver, except with the Ithaca M37, in which the trigger assembly slides out the rear when the pins and screws are disengaged.

The barrel can be removed from most models (again the Nova is the exception) by unscrewing the magazine cap, drawing back the bolt, and turning the barrel until it releases. With most pumps the magazine cap is "unscrewed" counterclockwise. The Ithaca M37, however, is turned clockwise since it must be lowered to draw it out of the barrel lug, freeing the barrel. Ithaca's DeerSlayer II and Storm models have fixed barrels that can't be removed for cleaning.

You'll usually need a spanner wrench to remove the forend from the magazine tube on virtually any pump gun.

To remove the trigger assembly on most pumps and autoloaders, simply take out the pins that run through the receiver. In rare instances, the assemblies are held in place with bolts.

AUTOLOADERS

The autoloader offers the quickest repeating action, firing a round, ejecting the spent hull, and replacing it in the chamber with a loaded one on each trip of the trigger.

These semiautomatics tame recoil better than any other action, using either an inertia block mechanical system or a gas piston to suppress the kick.

The drawbacks are that autoloaders are the heaviest shotguns made and the most expensive—barring high-end double guns. Autoloaders are also more complicated than other actions, often less reliable (particularly in tough field conditions), and somewhat less accurate for slug shooting due to the excessive vibration caused by the cycling action.

The John Browning–designed Auto-5, made from 1905 to 1997 (also the Remington Model 11 and Savage Model 720 under the same patent), is an American classic autoloader. The Remington 1100 is the lightest and oldest autoloading model on the market; it's available in 12-, 20-, 16-, and 28-gauge. Its successor, the 12-gauge 11–87, features an advanced gas-operated system in a heavier frame and optional 3½-inch chamber and comes in specialty versions for deer, turkey, and waterfowl hunters.

Browning's Gold (and its twin, the Winchester Super-X2), Benelli's 12-gauge Super Black Eagle and M1, and Beretta's 391 Urika and 12-gauge ES100 (formerly the Pintail and a more austere twin of the Benelli Super Black Eagle) are also popular.

The Remington 1100 autoloader comes in 12-, 16-, 20-, and 28-gauge.

To remove the barrel of an autoloader, start by unscrewing the magazine cap.

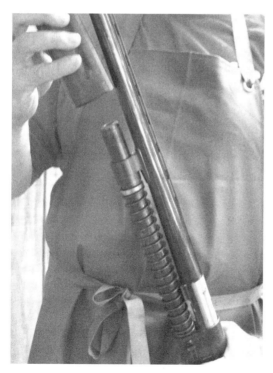

Then remove the forearm, which releases the barrel.

The Browning Auto-5 differs from most repeating shotguns in that its stock is held in place by a large crossbolt at the rear of the receiver, instead of a long stock bolt accessed through the buttstock.

Charles Daly, Franchi, Fabarms, and several other European actions are also available on the U.S. market.

The barrel on most autoloaders can be removed by locking the bolt back, putting pressure on the barrel toward the receiver, and unscrewing the magazine cap. The stock can be disengaged by pulling the recoil pad and loosening the long stock bolt inside the buttstock, except on the Browning Auto-5, which has a bolt that traverses the rear of the receiver that must be removed.

The complicated action on an autoloader is difficult to disassemble. Here again, both pins and screws are used to hold the action in place, and you'll find that some of these serve multiple functions while others are merely for structural support.

Most autoloaders can be torn down adequately, but it takes experience, knowledge, and usually schematics from the factory.

The Savage 210 is the only bolt-action, rifled-barrel shotgun still on the market.

BOLT ACTIONS

The bolt action is inexpensive, simple, and durable, but cycling the gun is cumbersome to the point of being useless for anything other than deer or turkey hunting, where single shots are the norm.

Today, the bolt action is state of the art in slug guns, but still no match in popularity for the omnipresent pump. Once among the least expensive and simplest shotgun actions, the addition of the rifled barrel and a few other amenities (like fiber-optic sights, rifle-style synthetic stocks, and scope mounts) has turned the bolt

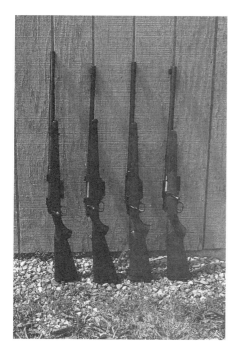

from a beginner's gun into the most inherently accurate slug gun available.

They are still a tough sell, however, as few models remain on the market. Savage, Marlin, and the Mossberg subsidiary of Maverick make the only production bolt-action shotguns today, and only the Savage 210 sports a rifled barrel.

Marlin's Model 55 goose gun, with its thirty-six-inch,

Slug guns with rifled barrels are very accurate.

12-gauge barrel, is unique. The Maverick model of the Mossberg line also offers a lower-priced bolt, smoothbore version of the parent firm's 695 rifled-barrel slug gun, which was discontinued in 2003. Marlin's 512 and Browning's A-Bolt rifled-barrel, bolt-action slug guns preceded the Mossberg 695 to pasture.

DOUBLE BARRELS

"Twice guns" are light and easy to point and carry and are considered the most romantic shotguns—classic wingshooting instruments.

Double guns are used almost exclusively by bird hunters and claybird shooters. Whether side-by-side or over-under, doubles offer an instant choice between two chokes and, in all but the lowest grades, excellent between-the-hands balance.

You won't find many deer hunters shooting doubles, with the possible exception of a tradition-bound Old South dog hunter using buckshot, mostly because barrels on double guns usually

have different points of aim and a deer gun is aimed rather than pointed as in wingshooting.

The side-by-side doubles, over the latter part of the twentieth century, gave way to the over-under in popularity. The over-under aims like a rifle, which in America—a nation of riflemen—may be part of its appeal.

Double-barrel shotguns have a nostalgic feel.

The most popular version in both side-by-side and over-under doubles is the boxlock, an action devised late in the nineteenth century that carries the trigger(s), sears, hammers, and attendant springs within the action body. The alternative is the sidelock, which carries the sear, hammer, mainspring, and tumbler on plates mounted on the sides of the action, inletted into the head of the stock and action bar.

The sidelock is a holdover from the days of flintlock and percussion-lock shotguns. The average sidelock has ten or more individual parts, while the modern boxlock uses just four. Most modern side-by-sides are boxlocks, which are more bulky but also more durable. High-dollar British gunmakers like Purdey and Holland & Holland still use sidelock actions.

A quality sidelock generally includes better trigger pulls than a boxlock and offers the added safety advantage of interceptor sears.

The drawbacks to doubles are their gaudy price tags and limited firepower, just one step above the hapless single shot. Ithaca, Winchester, Fox, Parker, and Remington made classic American

The over-under is the most popular type of double gun.

side-by-side doubles, but the Ruger Gold Label is the only American-made production side-by-side today. Weatherby and Savage offer models made offshore, as does Beretta and a variety of European gunmakers.

Prices range from three hundred dollars for the Cowboy Action-Darling Stoeger Coach Gun to thirty thousand or more for a high-grade Winchester, Fox, or Ithaca "reproduction."

Ruger and Remington make the only over-unders produced on these shores, but stack-barrel models built offshore are available through Browning, Winchester, Weatherby, Beretta, Benelli, Charles Daly, Fabarms, and others.

Today, all but the most expensive double guns use ejectors rather than extractors—meaning that spent hulls are jettisoned automatically when the gun is broken open instead of removed by hand. And the dainty "splinter" forends have, for the most part, been replaced by wider, bulkier versions on modern guns.

Doubles can almost universally be disassembled by working a lever to detach the forend, freeing the barrels to pivot downward and off the hinges of the action. It usually takes a practiced hand to fully disassemble the inner workings of a double, but simply removing the forend and barrels is usually sufficient for cleaning.

The receiver is often a sandwich of breechblock and upper tang, where the safety button is located. Unless you know the sequence of screws to remove, you may well loosen something that should actually stay tight. And putting it back together so that the safety linkage mates correctly with the button and bearing against the triggers can be frustrating if not mind-boggling.

Take it apart only if you have the proper instructions. With many older guns, however, there are no instructions, in which case it's best to have someone experienced with those guns do the disassembly and assembly—but expect to pay handsomely for that expertise.

There's rarely a need to disassemble the action on a side-by-side shotgun.

Pins and/or screws hold the action in place. Actions that utilize a stock bolt must be disassembled by first removing the bolt
and stock. To find out if your double has a stock bolt, remove the
recoil pad and look for a large diameter hole drilled lengthwise in
the stock with a bolt head in the dark recess.

SINGLE SHOTS

Single shots are by far the simplest, least expensive shotgun actions. They also kick harder than any other gun, and follow-up
shots are problematical at best.

Single-shot, break-open guns are built by H&R and New
England Firearms, Mossberg, and Thompson/Center. H&R and
New England Firearms, which are now owned by Marlin, offer
entry-level and specialty single-shot guns that range in price from
less than one hundred dollars in the Tracker version to the 12-
and 10-gauge turkey models at around three hundred dollars.

The H&R 980 is a bull-barreled, single-shot slug gun.

Mossberg's SSi-ONE is actually an interchangeable barrel design, as is the T/C Encore. The latter is a modification of a popular pistol design.

There is seldom a need to disassemble a single-shot receiver — in fact, I never have. The receiver is well sealed against the elements.

Detach the forend in the same manner you would a double barrel (using a screw or lever, depending on the model), then fold the barrel down and detach it from the receiver. This exposes all the surfaces that need to be cleaned: the barrel (inside and out), water table, breech face, and hinge pin. The stock can be detached from the receiver by removing the butt plate or recoil pad and loosening the stock bolt within.

If the gun has been dunked in water and interior rust is a concern, immerse the receiver-action in a jar of oil or solvent and let it soak. Then drain it completely and wipe it off. If you are working with a water-based cleaner, use a hair dryer or heat gun to dry it as thoroughly as possible.

CLASSIC AMERICAN DOUBLES

A. H. Fox, Parker Brothers, Remington, Winchester, and Ithaca Gun doubles faded to black in the 1940s due to the escalating cost of skilled labor in the face of automation. But nostalgia sells, and later there were some attempts at reproducing the classics. Remington and other companies brought out Parker reproductions; Marlin did a modestly priced L. C. Smith sequel; U.S. Repeating Arms kept the Winchester 21 alive; and Ithaca Gun's NID survived through their custom shops into the 1950s.

Some true, American-made "classics" still exist for those with sufficient passion and disposable income. Regrettably, they are called "reproductions," which somehow implies that they are cheap imitations. That is an unfounded and unfair perspective often prevalent in the shotgun world. What is a reproduction and what is an original shotgun is subject to some interpretation and can be further clouded by semantics.

In reality, today's reproductions are built in America by updated companies to exactly the same (although more consistent) specs as the originals. Modern metals, manufacturing methods, and finishes actually make them better than the one-offs. Honestly, aren't all American firearms built by something other than the original companies? Why aren't they all called reproductions?

As of this writing, only the Fox and Winchester 21 are still in production.

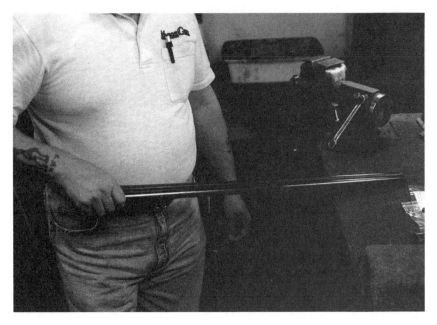

Tapping a set of barrels on a work surface reveals whether the rib is solid or needs soldering.

PURCHASING A USED SHOTGUN

It takes a lot of experience, but anyone interested in gun-smithing should know how to evaluate a used gun. Is the shot-gun lightly used or well cared for or fit only for hanging on the wall?

Fit and finish are matters of personal preference. To me, a shotgun is a tool; if it fits and functions correctly—or can be adjusted to function correctly—I don't care much about the finish or initial fit. Other shotgunners may actually look for "beat" guns so that they can primp them up for resale or personal use.

The first thing I check is the action. Is it tight? Does it function crisply without slop or stiffness? Does it lock up solidly? If it's a double, is there a gap between the barrels and the face? Are the hinge pins worn and sloppy? If you get a chance, remove the barrels and bang them against a tabletop. If they "ping," they're tight. But if they rattle, the rib is loose and it may or may not be fixable by soldering. If the gun has much age on it, chances are it's not worth fixing the rib.

I also check for barrel fit in used pumps and autoloaders, particularly if the latter is a recoil-operated firearm where the barrel slides back into the receiver as part of the cycling process. Excessive wear cannot be fixed, but it's rare that a shotgun gets that much use these days.

Check the interior of the barrel. If it's pitted, a good polishing job will usually clean it up—if the rest of the gun is worth the investment. If the barrel has a dent, that too can be raised. Even a bent barrel shouldn't deter you from looking at an otherwise sound shotgun. A gunsmith with some training and the correct jig can fix this if the bend isn't too severe. I certainly don't recommend it, but I've actually seen trapshooters bend barrels between rounds of competition by wedging them between truck bodies and bumpers.

You probably won't be able to dry fire the shotgun you're examining, but of course, that wouldn't tell you about anything except trigger pull anyway. If you're looking at old doubles, check the barrels first. If there is a gap around the rib, chances are the barrel was shortened to remove the chokes. If the gun has twist steel or Damascus steel (similar in appearance) barrels, don't buy it for anything but hanging on the wall. I've seen a few daredevils put light smokeless powder loads through them, but those guns were made to withstand blackpowder pressures only, not the pressures of modern loads.

GREENER'S RULE OF NINETY-SIX

British gunbuilder William Wellington Greener was not only an innovative designer, but also a respected researcher and author. His 1881 work, *The Gun and Its Development,* is a classic that is still used as a reference book today.

The book introduced a standard that is known as "Greener's Rule of Ninety-Six." Simply stated, Greener's calculations showed that a shotgun should be ninety-six times heavier than the weight of the shot charge it fires in order to ensure good patterns, the shooter's comfort, and the longevity of the firearm.

Applying this rule, a shotgun firing one ounce of shot should weigh six pounds. A load of 1⅛ ounces is better suited for a 6¾-pound gun; 7½-pound guns are needed to handle 1¼-ounce loads. Of the many pronouncements made by early gunmakers, this one is generally accepted as gospel, which means that today's outsized loads are way out of whack.

For instance, Greener's theory would dictate that the brutal but popular 3½-inch 12-gauge of today would require a 13½-pound gun to handle its current 2¼-ounce payload.

Chapter 4

___

BARRELS

We all know that the barrel (or barrels) of a shotgun is the tube that contains and directs shot toward the target. And the chamber, at the breech end, is the portion of the barrel that holds the unfired shell in position for detonation.

There is a forcing cone immediately forward of the chamber, an area that tapers down gradually from chamber diameter to barrel diameter. Its function is to provide a smooth transition for the ejecta wad, shot, and gas from the chamber into the barrel.

Three to seven inches from the muzzle another forcing cone starts, this one opening from barrel diameter to choke diameter. The choke constriction shapes the shot charge. Extending the forcing cones somewhat eases the trauma on the shot charge, giving it more room for the individual pellets to sort themselves out before traversing the tube. This also reduces felt recoil and improves pellet pattern due to the decreased number of deformed pellets.

In older barrels—those made before the advent of plastic, gas-sealing wads—the chamber forcing cones are often short and abrupt, maybe ⅜ to 1 inch in length with a 5- to 7-degree taper. Newer designs offer 1½- to 3-inch forcing cones, which provide a longer, more gentle transition for the shot column.

Backbored, or over-bored, barrels are common on custom turkey and waterfowl guns (although their functionality is dubious).

Shotgun barrels are now cut from solid steel blanks on computerized milling machines rather than hot-forged by hammering over mandrels.

They can be found in Browning Gold and BPS and Winchester Super-X2 12-gauge guns (Invector Plus), as well as in Mossberg's 835 Ultri-Mag and some European guns. A backbored barrel offers a much larger interior diameter, designed to allow an easier passage for the shot charge with less pellet deformity, more consistent patterning, and less felt recoil.

Backbored 12-gauge barrels commonly sport interior diameters in the 0.735- to 0.740-inch range. The term also applies to barrels that have longer forcing cones at the breech and muzzle, which serve the same purpose.

Having counted more than a few little holes in patterning targets, I can honestly say that I haven't seen any better performance from backbored barrels than from those with extended forcing cones. In fact, gunmakers tell me that chamber forcing cones longer than three inches do not provide any additional benefit.

This water-driven barrel reamer has been in operation at the Ithaca Gun plant since before World War I.

Virtually all pump and autoloading guns are available in versions with a raised rib and at least a single bead sight or with optional rifle-sighted slug-shooting version. Modern bolt-action and single-shot guns will not feature raised ribs since they are essentially slug or turkey guns that require rifle sights (often fiber optic) for aiming rather than pointing.

BARREL LENGTH AND FEATURES

In my youth, I often heard about a shotgun known as the "Long Tom," usually a long-barreled, single-shot 12-gauge that was purported to turn a gallon bucket into door screen at sixty yards. Probably an exaggeration, but at one time the long barrels were necessary to fully burn the powders of the day and provide magnum velocity and energy.

Today's smokeless powders burn in the first few inches of the barrel, and the rest of the tube simply orients the charge toward the target. Longer barrels do provide slightly higher velocities, but only until about twenty-five inches. The velocities level off at that point and actually start to drop with extremely long barrels, which apparently act as a brake due to friction.

The reign of the Long Tom as king of American shotgunning passed a couple of decades ago. Long (30- to 32-inch) barrels faded in popularity in favor of shorter, lighter shotguns that were easier to tote afield yet yielded surprising comparable ballistics. The long barrels weren't ineffective, they just didn't fit the needs of modern shotgunners as well.

But the long barrel is making a strong comeback today, particularly among sporting-clays enthusiasts who see 30-inch barrels as a bare necessity and 32- or 34-inchers as perfect.

The fact remains that barrel length is an integral part of wingshooting dynamics. The longer barrel's improved sighting plane is one factor, but probably the biggest reason is that the inertia involved in swinging a longer barrel makes for a smoother swing and more certain follow-through. It simply improves a shooter's form. Maybe the old-timers had the right idea all along.

It also should be noted, though, that the tightest-patterning shotguns in existence, those built for "card-shooting," which pro-

Skeet shooters prefer long barrels that swing smoothly.

duces ragged one-hole patterns a couple of inches wide, have no forcing cones and no choke constriction at all. They are also extremely long, often in excess of 60 inches, which allows the pellets sufficient time to get in an orderly line while still in the confines of the tube. In essence, the shot string is formed before it leaves the barrel, resulting in an extremely uniform flight for all the pellets.

You'll also find that non-American shotguns normally have a true bore diameter of approximately 0.005 inch less than U.S. standard barrels (generally a true bore diameter of 0.725), which of course makes a difference when choosing a choke constriction.

English barrels are notoriously thin and whippy—0.02-inch wall thickness for 2- and 2½-inch chambers and 0.025 for 2¾-inch guns. American barrels are overbuilt up to 0.035 inch. Belgian, German, French, and Italian barrels follow the American logic.

It should be noted that "porting" a barrel—having holes drilled in the barrel ahead of the muzzle—vents gases in a specific direction and tends to reduce barrel jump and felt recoil. This is partly why so many specialty guns have ported barrels and why many extended choke tubes are ported.

Shotguns made in the early twentieth century often have 2½-inch chambers that must be lengthened to accept modern loads.

In addition to reducing barrel jump, ports are known to grab and slow the shotcup, which helps separate it from the shot column. This keeps the shotcup-wad from blowing into the pattern and tends to shorten the shot string for better pattern density.

While porting a barrel has advantages, the sound pressure wave delivered to the shooter's face and ear is greatly increased. Extensive testing has shown that porting increases the report's noise level by at least 8 decibels, which may not sound like much, but it represents an increase of 60 percent in the sound pressure magnitude. That's obviously significant.

OPTIMUM LENGTH

European gunmakers long followed the British dictum that a shotgun's barrel length should be forty times its bore diameter. That means a 12-gauge gun with a 0.729-inch bore needed a 29.16-inch barrel, 30 inches being a reasonable compromise from a manufacturing perspective.

Americans, on the other hand, have long cut barrels based on comfort and use. A 26- or 28-inch barrel on a

Sporting-clays competitors often choose barrels as long as 30 to 34 inches.

field gun, regardless of action, usually affords sufficient balance and inertia for smooth barrel swing without constantly catching on brush.

Claybird shooters, however, don't worry about brush or carrying the gun and prefer the smooth-swinging characteristics (even at the sacrifice of precise balance) offered by thirty- to 34-inch barrels. Turkey hunters and slug shooters who aim their guns rather than point and swing, are perfectly happy with stubby 20- to 24-inch barrels that are easier to lug around and maneuver through brush.

BARREL MODIFICATIONS

Barrel modifications are among the most frequently requested shotgun gunsmithing jobs, but they may also be the least warranted and the most often screwed up. A gunsmith should always keep this in mind when issuing advice or commencing work on a barrel.

In particular, altering forcing cones is quite popular, but there is little to be gained. This is not to say that lengthening a forcing cone will not improve the performance of a barrel. It may, but then again, it may not be necessary and, if done improperly, can definitely be detrimental to the barrel's performance.

In the last section, we discussed the fact that there is a forcing cone at each end of the barrel. In most American-made shotguns, the initial forcing cone—the one that follows the chamber—is a ½-inch in length. The sharp angle of the cone walls provides quite a bit of resistance to the passage of the charge. In soft pellet loads like lead, that can mean more pellet deformation. Lengthening the cone to 1½ inches significantly

reduces the resistance and the deformation of the pellets, effectively lessening recoil and increasing pattern density.

So, lengthening the forcing cone is a good thing, right?
Well, yes. Provided the ream job is straight and necessary, it's one
of the hottest barrel modifications offered by performance-ori-
ented gunsmiths today.

But there is a lot of smoke and mirrors in this type of work.
Many smiths, probably working from ballistic ignorance, feel
that longer is better and may ream cones out to five inches or
more. Much research has been done on the matter, and it's been
found that there is absolutely no benefit in lengthening a cone to
more than 1½ to 1¾ inches. In fact, you'll find that many high-
end modern shotguns, particularly target-shooting models, now
come from the factory with 1½-inch forcing cones, and I'm willing

to bet that lengthening
them will provide virtu-
ally no improvement in
recoil or patterning.

Now, the average
shotgunner won't even
know the length of the
forcing cone in his bar-
rel unless he asks cus-
tomer service at the
factory. Most gunsmiths,
in fact, don't know until
they measure. Using in-
side calipers to measure
the diameter will tell
you where the chamber

Measuring chamber length.

ends. Experienced hands can simply run a straight gauge (metal ruler) down the chamber walls and feel the point where the forcing cone starts, marking the head of the chamber. Shops that deal with a lot of older guns may actually mill, cast, or mold a go/no-go plug to insert in a chamber to quickly determine length.

Lengthening a forcing cone beyond 1½ inches is overkill. And if the cone is reamed crooked it will weaken the barrel. The barrel wall will be thinned at a critical point on one side, which can cause pellet deformation and poor patterns.

The best way to lengthen a forcing cone is to hand-ream it with the barrel held absolutely vertical and level. The reamer must be run absolutely concentric with the bore, and you can't stop the process and then start again.

It takes "feel" to efficiently hand-ream a barrel. It's all in the pressure applied—too light and the reamer will skid and not cut, too heavy and the reamer will cut too deep and stall. The optimum pressure allows a steady grinding feel.

The whole procedure can actually be completed with a lathe, drill press, or even a hand drill, but there's no feel involved. And if it's reamed crooked, redoing the job can be difficult because the metal might have been tempered (hardened) by the friction heat from the high-speed application.

You may have heard that lengthening a forcing cone is necessary for better steel-shot (or tungsten-iron) performance because these loads have higher chamber pressures and their hardness leads to barrel scoring if the passage of the charge isn't relieved a bit.

That's totally false. First, the harder loads don't produce higher chamber pressures than lead. And even if they did, lengthening the cone would have no effect on that. In fact, lengthening the forcing cone, which requires removing metal from the interior of the barrel, only serves to weaken the barrel at that point, not strengthen it.

And steel or tungsten pellets won't score the barrel because with today's thick plastic wads, the pellets never even touch the barrel—they travel from the chamber through the length of the barrel and out the choke completely enveloped in the plastic tube. The pattern size is determined by the amount of drag the choke constriction puts on the wad (shotcup).

Many shotgunners were advised, and probably accepted as gospel, that they shouldn't shoot steel or tungsten-iron (and now Hevi-Shot) through older barrels because of high pressures and the inevitable scoring by the harder pellets. Many wonderful Model 12s were retired and Browning Auto-5 barrels replaced by "savvy" waterfowlers concerned with ruining their favorite barrels—including me on the latter score. But the truth is that it simply wasn't, and isn't, a problem.

Granted, in the early days of steel shot when ammunition manufacturers really didn't know what they were doing, some steel pellets might have escaped shotcups and scored barrels. Or in cases where the bore was radically oversized (backbored), pellets could conceivably have slipped through slits in the wad and contacted the barrel walls. But these problems have pretty much been eliminated by today's ultra-efficient shotcups.

The bottom line is that lengthening a forcing cone to 1½ inches may provide a slight improvement in small-pellet lead patterns, but it will do nothing for steel or exotic shot patterning, and it would take an imaginative mind to notice any reduction in recoil.

Over-boring or backboring, essentially extending the forcing cone from the chamber to the choke constriction by opening the barrel diameter several thousandths of an inch beyond the norm, has been touted for waterfowlers using steel and exotic shot, for turkey hunters seeking tight, long-range patterns, and for buckshot shooters. But it's a very expensive process, beyond the capability of machinery in most gun shops, and as mentioned earlier, it really doesn't serve much purpose.

It will produce a more uniform pattern for small-shot applications like target shooting and will probably reduce perceived recoil. But it does not help waterfowl, turkey, or buckshot patterns—at least not for the reasons you've probably been told.

If the big- or hard-shot patterns are improved by backbored barrels, it's because the increased elbowroom in the barrel has compromised the load. Having a bigger tunnel to traverse tends to lessen velocity since the propellant gases aren't as well contained; they slip past the charge. The slower charge may pattern better, but trading down in velocity for added comfort is usually a bad idea for shooters.

And, as mentioned previously, the larger internal diameter may allow pellets to slip between the wad petals and contact the bore, which means worse patterning with lead loads (more deformed pellets) and possible barrel scoring with hard pellets.

If someone demands that a barrel be backbored to a specific dimension, say 0.765 inch, which is often recommended for recoil reduction, make sure you measure the internal barrel dimension with calipers before starting work on the gun.

You will find all manner of internal diameters in guns from the factory, very few at the nominal 12-gauge specification of 0.729 inch. My 1960s Browning Auto-5 measures 0.722, my new Beretta 391 mikes in the 0.718 neighborhood, and I've seen Mossberg 500s at 0.732.

Polishing a bore makes a lot more sense than backboring or radically lengthening the forcing cone. This just means that about 0.003 inch or less of metal inside the barrel is removed in order to give it a mirror-smooth finish. Polishing can be done to remove pitting or earlier tool marks, and it discourages rust and plastic buildup from shotcups and decreases friction when the charge traverses the tube. A good polish job will often increase small-pellet lead patterns by several percentage points.

Chrome-lining a barrel is another option that achieves approximately the same results as a good polishing job, but it's much more expensive and makes any future work on the barrel prohibitive. Most gunsmiths won't attempt to ream or install a screw-in choke system in a chrome-lined barrel because the chrome is very hard and may flake out or have to be removed entirely to work on the barrel itself. Chrome-lining, or removing chrome, is a difficult procedure that must be farmed out to specialists.

Barrel porting is another very popular barrel modification these days. Putting ports (holes) in the barrel, usually near the muzzle, is accomplished by drilling through the barrel walls or etching slots through the walls by electrolysis or chemical action. Regardless of the porting method, the barrel should be re-blued to protect against corrosion.

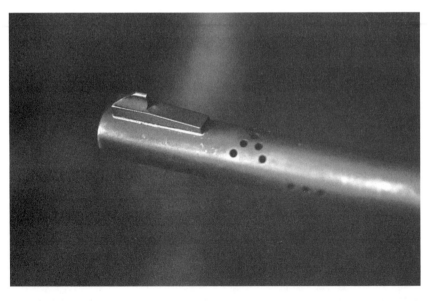

Porting a barrel lessens felt recoil and reduces barrel jump, but makes the shotgun's report much louder.

U-Port-It barrel porting jig.

Virtually anyone with the right drill bits, a drill press, and a porting jig can port a barrel, but care must be taken to polish off the resultant burrs in the barrel's interior. Given the low price— less than a hundred dollars in most cases—of having a specialty shop do the porting and re-blueing, it usually isn't worth the effort to do it yourself. Chemical etching is a much more sophisticated operation that is well beyond the skills or equipment of a small shop.

Most folks want their barrels ported because they've heard that it reduces recoil. It actually reduces what is known as "perceived recoil," but the laws of physics make it impossible to reduce the actual rearward momentum of the gun by drilling holes in it. A gun of a specific mass will react in a specific manner with predictable force when a specific-sized charge is ignited, and no amount of venting the barrel will reduce that force.

Actual recoil, the rearward thrust of the gun upon ignition of the charge, is only one factor in perceived recoil. Other factors include barrel jump and how hard the stock slams your cheek, as well as how loud the report is. Science aside, perceived recoil is what the shooter is actually concerned with.

How hard your cheek gets slapped can largely be controlled by how the gun fits you. But for reducing muzzle jump, the positioning of the ports on the barrel is critical. They should be cut in the top of the barrel, as close to the muzzle as possible. (Cutting them in the sides of the barrel doesn't net the desired results.)

If you're working on an over-under double, it doesn't make sense to perforate both barrels. Since porting is done to combat muzzle jump, it's really only effective for the first shot in a two-shot gun. The top barrel is usually fired first, and there is an obvious advantage in porting it because holes can be cut in the very top, better directing down force against barrel jump, whereas the top of the lower barrel is not accessible.

Porting, when done correctly, generally does reduce barrel jump significantly. But it bleeds off gases before they reach the muzzle, which may reduce pressures to the point that a gas-operated semiautomatic will not cycle.

REAMING AND POLISHING

Rick Hammond of Newark Valley, New York, specializes in old double barrels and does almost all the metal work by hand, maintaining that "these guns were built with hand tools, they should be repaired with them."

In my formative years in gunsmithing it was Rick who taught me how to hand-ream chambers and forcing cones. Actually, I received complete instructions with the reamers from Brownells, but his hands-on mentoring was invaluable. It started when I bought a tight, well-balanced 1922 Ithaca Flues 16-gauge double as a bird-hunting gun. But I'd been told that the Flues models were not shootable and that the short chambers could not be safely altered.

The gun had been restocked with very nice wood and case hardened by someone who obviously knew what he was doing, and the chokes had been reamed to modified and improved cylinder from their original full and full. Given the amount of work that had been done on the gun, I had Rick check to see if

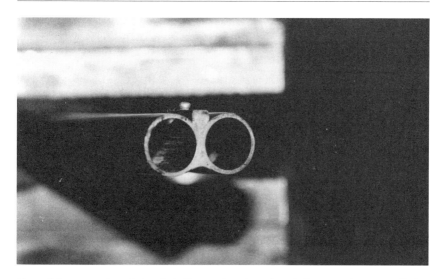

The solid cross-section of the rib indicates that these barrels have not been cut off, but the reamer marks inside the bore will need to be polished with a hone.

the chambers had been lengthened (at that point, I didn't even know how to check chamber length) from the original 2½ inches to 2¾ to accommodate modern loads. Surprisingly, they hadn't. Nor had the forcing cones been extended from the original abrupt half-inch, but Rick said that both could be lengthened safely. He strongly disagreed with the advice I'd been given, stating that the gun certainly could be a shooter and agreeing to do the work while teaching me in the process.

HAND-REAMING CHAMBERS

Start the chamber-lengthening process by clamping the barrel, chamber up, in a vise, making sure the breech opening is absolutely level. Brush cutting oil onto the reamer, and slide it down the barrel.

Hand-reaming is fairly simple, but it does take practice and the "feel" I alluded to earlier. Turn the T-handle while pressing down gently until the reamer bites steel. The amount of pressure

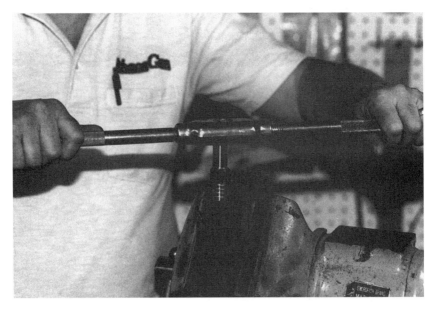

Lengthening a forcing cone or chamber with a hand reamer is not difficult if you follow instructions carefully.

necessary will vary. If you don't press hard enough the reamer won't bite, sliding over the surface instead. Too much pressure will make the reamer bite too deeply and stall.

Perfect pressure makes a smooth grating sound and a smooth, consistent bite that you can feel. Rotate the reamer twice, then pull it out while maintaining the clockwise turn—do not reverse.

Brush the reamer and chamber clean of chips and measure your progress. Continue oiling, reaming, and checking the progress until your chamber gauge rests in the chamber with the front edge of the groove touching the rear of the chamber. Scrub the chamber clean.

Now install a barrel hone in the chuck of your drill. Clamp the barrel in a horizontal position and place some lubricating oil in the chamber. Hone back and forth in the chamber, then wipe it clean; it has been polished.

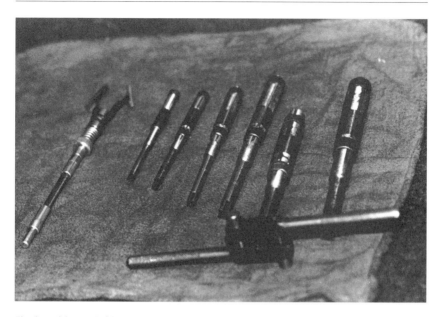

The barrel hone (left) polishes the barrel's interior after the reamers do their work.

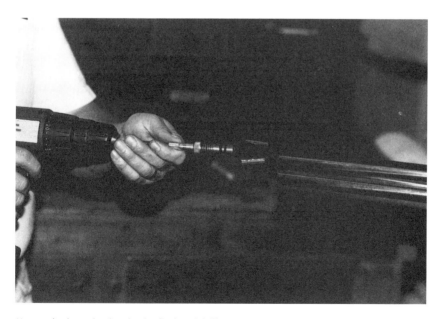

Mount the hone in the chuck of a hand drill.

Extending the forcing cone is accomplished in a similar manner and with the same reamer.

A flex hone (with its special oil) is the best instrument for polishing the forcing cone or the entire length of the bore. Mount it in a variable-speed drill, wet the bore with the special oil (do not use a substitute or the hone will disintegrate), and push the hone into the desired area at slow speed. Run the hone three or four times, then remove it. If you feel the need, start with a medium-grit hone and repeat the process with a fine-grit—but a newer barrel will need only the fine-grit.

REMOVING DENTS

Removing dents from a barrel is a common shotgun repair. Today, the best way to do this is with a hydraulic dent lifter.

Dents can still be removed the old way, by driving a tapered plug down the bore, but you may scratch the bore, and the plug may not exactly match the bore diameter. These considerations make most gunsmiths shy away from this method. So if you want to handle these repairs, you'll have to invest in a dent lifter, which is gauge-specific and not inexpensive.

Start by marking the dent on the outside of the barrel. Then mark the handle of the lifter in line with the lifting pad of the hydraulic head. Now hold the lifter next to the barrel and slide the locking collar until it stops at the muzzle (or breech, if you're working from that direction). The collar stops the lifting pad at the dent, so it's important to get the collar just right before locking it in place.

On the rear of the handle you'll find the expansion bolt. Run the bolt out and press the lifting pad down with your thumb until it fits into the barrel. Run an oily patch down the bore, and then clamp the barrel in a vise with the dent visible.

Slide the hydraulic lifter into the bore and line up the handle mark with the dent. Tighten the expansion bolt with an

Allen wrench. When the lifting pad contacts the dent, the bolt will become difficult to turn.

The expansion bolt tries to compress the hydraulic fluid in the rod, but the fluid is formulated to resist, which makes the lifting pad rise. Since the lifting pad is smaller than the opposite side of the lifter head, compound leverage is applied to the dent.

Carefully turn the expansion bolt a little at a time until the dent is raised. Stop here or you will bulge the barrel. Loosen the expansion bolt and remove the tool from the barrel. If the dent has been raised unevenly, you may have to reposition the tool and repeat the process two or three times.

To remove the dent's last traces, loosen the locking collar and pull the lifter away from the dent while gently tightening the expansion nut. When the lifting pad reaches the bore, don't press on it—you've just turned it into a bore gauge. Slide the tool back and forth through the dent location. If it stops, move the locking collar a half-inch from the end of the barrel and lock it in place. Loosen the expansion nut and slide the tool until the collar stops it. Tighten the expansion nut; you won't need to turn it more than a little past contact with the dent.

Use a barrel hone to polish and clean the newly repaired area.

INSTALLING SHOTGUN BEADS

It's often necessary to exchange or remove and remount front beads or new sights. This is a fairly simple procedure, although it has dangerous consequences when done incorrectly. If the bead's shank extends into the bore of the shotgun, the shooter will be lucky if only the barrel gets damaged upon firing. But with a few simple tools and a willingness to follow proven procedures, you shouldn't have any trouble.

If you have to remove a bead, just grip it with pliers (with padded jaws if the bead is to be reused or saved) and unscrew the

Forster universal sight mounting fixture.

threaded shank. If it's stubborn—and it undoubtedly will be if you are in a hurry or if you offered to do the job for free—apply a good penetrating oil. I like Liquid Wrench or WD-40. Apply it per the instructions, give the bead a light tap, and then let it sit ten or fifteen minutes. The bead should come right off on the next attempt.

If the bead was broken off and the shank is still in the hole, it must be drilled out and a new thread tapped. Beads customarily come in sizes 3–56, 4–40, or the larger 6–48 and range in diameter from 0.067 to 0.175 inch. You'll need a No. 28 or No. 31 drill and taps with the same threads.

Use a short bit when drilling, as longer bits tend to flex and wander. It's best to have both taper and bottom taps in each size. The taper is used to tap a hole through the barrel, while the bottom tap—if used properly—keeps the bead's shank from going through the barrel and into the bore.

Conventional bead types include steel, brass, aluminum, or plastic, all available in ten-packs. Brownells sells more comprehensive kits with several of each variety, which just about assures you of an exact match if you are replacing an existing bead. Ithaca-style Raybar, Simmons Glow Worms, or variations of the new colored fiber-optic sights are also available.

If you need to drill a new hole, a drill jig makes the operation virtually foolproof. B-Square makes a nice barrel-sight drill jig that consists of a precision V-block drill guide with

Brownells shotgun sight installer.

two No. 31 bushings located 0.5625 inch apart. It can be used for both front and rear sights, which is handy for putting Tru-Glo, Williams, HiViz, or any other two-piece fiber-optic sets on a deer or turkey gun. Just follow the instructions that come with the jig.

Once the hole is drilled, tap it with a hand tap and tap guide and the appropriate amount of Tap Magic cutting oil. Once the hole is drilled, tapped, and cleaned, be sure you have the appropriate shank thread—too big and it'll jam, too small and the sight will wobble and eventually fall off.

Start the new bead by hand or with the popular bead installation tool from Brownells. If the hole goes all the way through the barrel wall, be sure that the screw shank does not protrude into the bore. If it does, remove it and grind it shorter on a grinding wheel.

Chapter 5

CHOKES

The advent of smokeless powder shotshells, which made multiple shots quicker and easier, brought about more sophisticated shotgun barrels that were reamed at the muzzle to a specific diameter. The amount of constriction varied with the intended use. A wider spread to the pattern helped for short-range shooting and a denser dispersion of shot for longer shots.

Several men are credited with originating the choke system. An Illinois duck hunter by the name of Fred Kimble claimed to have invented the concept in 1867. American gunsmith Sylvester Roper received patent approval on a screw-in choke system in 1866, just six weeks before British designer William Rochester Pape filed a similar patent. Still others claim that choke systems were Spanish or French ideas. The earliest claimant on these shores appears to be Rhode Island gunsmith Jeremiah Smith, who "discovered the merits of choke boring in 1827," according to an early issue of *American Wildfowling* magazine.

Regardless of who invented it, choke boring changed the face of shotgunning. Today, the undisputed king of the choke tube is Texan Jess Briley. The Houston machinist developed choke tubes in his garage shop in the mid-1970s and now turns out more than a million units a year under a wide variety of brand names, controlling nearly 90 percent of the market.

The nominal bore size for a 12-gauge shotgun is 0.729 inch in diameter. But the choke constrictions vary slightly in designation between lead and steel (or nontoxic shot). A 12-gauge barrel with no constriction (cylinder bore) is 0.729. A constriction of 0.724 is considered a skeet choke for lead shooters. Improved-cylinder (0.009 constriction or 0.720 diameter) for lead, however, is actually considered a skeet choke for nontoxic loads.

Conventional constriction for a 12-gauge skeet II choke is 0.012 and for modified choke it is 0.019 (or a 0.710 bore diameter). The latter is the same dimension considered improved cylinder for steel shot. An improved-modified conventional choke is 0.704 (0.025 constriction), which converts to extra-full for steel shot.

Be advised, however, that all of these measurements are specs,  labels. All shotgun bores, particularly older ones, vary slightly in internal diameter, which is why a choke tube will pattern differently when screwed into different barrels. The degree of choke in a barrel is simply a measure of constriction from the bore to the muzzle. Since interior barrel dimensions can vary by as much as 0.02 inch from gun to gun, there is a better way of determining choke.

Double guns, which offer two choices of choke, are popular with upland bird hunters.

The true choke size is determined by the difference between the diameter of the bore relative to the diameter of the constriction. By subtracting the diameter of the choke from that of the bore you will be able to determine the amount of constriction (choke) you have, regardless of the roll-stamp on the barrel. This measurement is what really counts.

For instance, if you have a choke tube that is cylinder relative to your 0.728 bore, the choke will be modified if used in a barrel of 0.742. But if your barrel's interior diameter measures 0.732, that same choke tube would represent cylinder bore.

For another illustration, let's go back to industry specs. A full choke in conventional terms is 0.694, or a constriction of 0.035, the same dimensions considered a modified choke for steel. Extra-full, usually reserved for turkey hunting with lead shot, is 0.040 constriction, or a 12-gauge bore diameter of 0.689.

Always measure the interior diameter of a barrel before selecting a particular constriction to fit the needs of a particular gun.

CONSTRICTION IS JUST PART OF IT

So, how does the microscopic 0.030- to 0.035-inch difference between a truly tight choke and a wide-open boring make such a marked difference in shot dispersion? Well, that tiny difference in diameter in itself doesn't much matter. It couldn't. The answer is that the choke is just one part of a complex system that orders pattern development.

Choke constriction does play an important role, but just as vital are a pair of dynamic forces that work in concert with the constriction to shape the shot charge before setting it free. The first factor is the pressure of the trailing wad on the base of the shot charge as it clears the muzzle, and the second is the air resistance (drag) that works against pellets once they escape the controlling wad and powder gases.

The pellets, encased in the plastic shotcup, go from a standing start in the chamber to a 1,200-feet-per-second (fps) mass in about 0.003 of a second. That puts a lot of pressure and momentum on the wad and pellets. The wad encounters the choke taper, which constricts it slightly from 0.0729 down to 0.695 in a full-choked barrel. That, again, is not much. But the tight choke does pinch down on the wad, slowing it and letting the shot charge escape with little or no pressure from the wad.

At the other extreme, a cylinder-bore or improved-cylinder choke pretty much lets the wad slide through without being bothered, meaning it can remain nestled up against the base of the shot charge. A modified choke gives the wad a slightly tighter squeeze, and improved-modified comes down almost as hard as the aforementioned full choke.

Thus, the way choke constriction slows the wad pretty much determines how the shot emerges from the muzzle, at which point it encounters air resistance. Air works harder against fast-

Dove shooters usually want an open choke.

moving objects than against slower ones, and the pellets slow abruptly during the first few feet out of the muzzle.

Pattern and shot-string formation depend on how powerful that rear wad pressure is. If it's heavy, as in the case of an improved-cylinder choke, the charge is virtually pancaked between the opposing forces of wad pressure and air resistance, and the pellets spread outward, widening the pattern.

In a full choke the wad is slowed more noticeably. The choke constriction retards the wad, and the pellet string narrows down to squeeze through the smaller opening. Pellets tend to spurt through a full choke because the narrowing is a minor obstruction. They thus escape in a longer line, and since the wad is delayed by the choke taper, the pellets continue on a straighter course because they are not being rammed from behind, as in the case of the more open choke.

This phenomenon is more pronounced at high altitudes where air is lighter. Patterns are tighter across the board at altitude due to the reduction of the air resistance factor. In a vacuum, an improved-cylinder choke would theoretically deliver patterns of 100 percent due to the absence of air resistance. The pellets could travel straight ahead, their superior mass giving them the momentum to outrun the wad and its potentially disruptive impact from behind.

Choke, then, is important only as it retards (or fails to retard) the wad, and in how it prepares the shot charge for its impact with air resistance.

CHOKE SYSTEMS

As noted, just a few thousandths of an inch difference in constriction can, for a variety of reasons, make a huge difference in pattern dispersion. The problem is that most shooting situations require different degrees of constriction. For a long time the only way to overcome the choke problem was to have more than one gun or to have another barrel or several barrels for one gun, which can be an expensive proposition. The average shooter was forced to adapt his shooting to the choke of his gun.

Choke sleeves that alter the constriction of the barrel at the muzzle have been around in one form or another for about 150 years, but it wasn't until around the midpoint of the twentieth century that shotguns with adjustable choke systems developed a strong presence in the marketplace.

Virtually all modern shotguns come with a screw-in choke tube system, but they are not universal. Manufacturers use different thread patterns and choke-tube dimensions. For instance, conventional Winchester, Browning, Ithaca, H&R, NEF, Weatherby, SKB, Savage, Smith & Wesson, Churchill, and most Ruger shotguns and Mossberg 500s and 9200s use Win-Choke thread systems, while Remington and 12-gauge Charles Daly autos are threaded for Rem-Choke systems.

Beretta, Benelli, and Franchi have their own Mobilchoke system. Browning and Winchester's backbored guns need Invector-

A screw-in choke tube makes any shotgun more versatile.

Plus choke tube systems, and the Mossberg 835 Ultri-Mag has a system of its own.

It's possible to change the chokes in a double gun without adding "modern" screw-in versions, but only if you are expanding an existing choke. (A hand reamer will do this job well.) No one can make a choke tighter without sleeving the entire barrel and starting over.

Choke	Ideal Range (in yards)	Effective Range (in yards)
Cylinder-Bore	15–22	10–27
Skeet I	20–27	15–32
Improved-Cylinder	25–32	20–37
Skeet II	30–37	25–42
Modified	35–42	30–47
Improved-Modified	40–47	35–52
Full	45–52	40–57
Extra-Full	50–57	45–62

INSTALLING SCREW-IN CHOKE SYSTEMS

Screw-in choke tubes give shotguns a remarkable versatility that has become the envy of countless owners of conventional, fixed-choke shotguns.

Thus, there is a steady aftermarket business for installing screw-in systems, if you have the expertise and equipment. Even if you are well equipped, you'll need to exercise careful judgment. If the gun is old or valuable, think before cutting.

Today's shotguns use 1040 steel in their receivers, while many older guns used milder 1020 steel. The pressure of modern hotter loads may not pose a dangerous problem, but you can't be sure—although you can be liable.

Not long ago it was virtually impossible for a gunsmith in a small shop to install a screw-in system. You needed to have a lathe with a bed long enough to accommodate the barrel, and the best bet was to send the barrel to a specialist.

But today specially designed hand tools can be used to make the necessary barrel modifications without a lathe. The tooling is costly, but it's definitely worth the investment if you perform this task on many guns. Colonial Arms and Clymer Manufacturing make the tooling.

IS THE BARREL SUITABLE?

To decide if a barrel is a good candidate for a screw-in choke tube, you must measure the bore diameter internally from the end of the forcing cone to the point where the choke begins at the barrel's end. If there is no choke constriction, the bore diameter is measured from the end of the forcing cone to the end of the barrel.

Is that bore diameter sufficient to allow choke installation? Select the steel pilot from the tooling kit that represents the maximum size for that gauge and insert it in the breech end of the barrel. If the pilot drops easily through the bore, that bore is too large to be fitted with choke tubes.

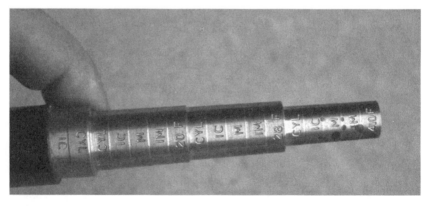

A drop-in gauge instantly tells you the choke of a particular barrel.

Colonial also has a maximum bore gauge. Insert it into the chamber and past the forcing cone. If it continues into the bore, you can't install a system in that barrel. The rule of thumb is that tube systems should not be installed in barrels with an internal diameter that exceeds 0.736 inch for 12-gauge; 0.730 for 12-gauge thinwall; 0.781 for 10-gauge; 0.668 for 16-gauge; 0.626 for 20-gauge; 0.560 for 28-gauge; and 0.416 for 410.

Before installing a system you must ascertain if the barrel wall thickness is sufficient to accept reaming and still handle ballistic pressures. Measure the barrel's outside diameter where the chokes would be installed, then measure the outside diameter of the tap. Subtract one from the other and divide that number in half to determine the remaining wall thickness. If that figure is less than 0.010 inch, forget the installation.

When taking these measurements, you must also consider the concentricity of the barrel. If the wall thickness varies at critical points the installation simply won't work, or the gun will be dangerous to use. Clymer actually makes a barrel-wall thickness gauge with a dial indicator to determine these measurements. The barrel is slipped over the gauge's contact ball and the indicator's plunger lowered to contact the barrel.

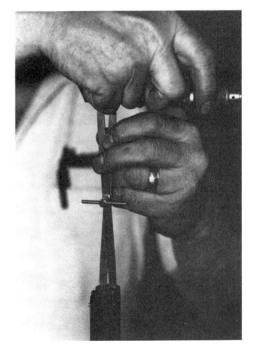

Wing (inside) calipers can measure choke diameter and depth.

MAKING THE CUT

Let's assume the barrel is suitable for the installation. Slide the barrel-seating spacer over the reamer until it stops on the reamer's largest dimension. The spacer is a small but very important part of the choke work because it will stop the reamer before the final choke seat is cut.

Now select the appropriate steel pilot—it should fit snugly in the bore without wobbling yet still turn freely. You'll know you have the right one when the next largest pilot won't even fit in the bore. Remember, if the pilot is too small the reamer will cut crookedly and the tubes will direct the charge to a different point of aim than the barrel point would indicate. This is something that happens regularly with some low-priced commercial barrels.

Insert the chosen pilot in the chamber end of the barrel, threaded end up, and push it down the bore. It will stop when

it hits the existing choke. Screw the end of the reamer into the pilot through the hole.

If the choke has been cut off the barrel, you'll have to use a bronze bushing from the kit that fits snugly but turns freely. Fit the bronze bushing to the reamer and insert it in the muzzle. Make sure the snap ring is in place as a stop.

Using a T-handled reamer to expand a choke.

You can use a hand-brace reamer or one mounted in a power drill that runs fifty to sixty rpm. Turn the reamer clockwise to gain ⅛ inch of depth, then withdraw it—still turning clockwise—to clean the chips and add oil to the bit. (Never reverse the reamer.) Keep repeating the process until you hit the stops.

The threading must be done by hand. Remove the spacer and install the tap on the same pilot or bushing used for the reaming. Lube the tap and slowly cut the threads into the barrel walls. It should cut smoothly, but stop after seventeen turns when it bottoms on the choke-seating surface.

Ease the cutter out of the threads to avoid damaging them, and then clean the bore again.

Now it's time to cut the choke. Switch back to the reamer and insert the tooling assembly into the bore. Oil the reamer and turn it clockwise to cut. Remove the reamer by continuing to turn it clockwise, clean off the chips, and check your progress with a good light. There should be a small gap between the seat and the section you just finished cutting.

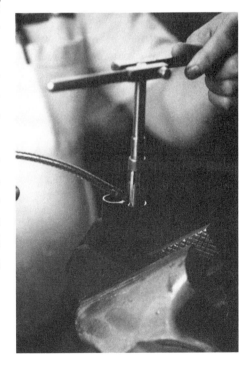

Clean the barrel with solvent and a bronze brush, then install an improved-cylinder tube. Check the seating at the muzzle and the interior (using a bore light).

Cutting oil is necessary whenever you ream a barrel.

It's a good idea to practice this installation process on scrap barrels several times before tackling the barrel on one of your favorites. Screw it up and it will cost you a barrel—or, if a flaw goes undetected in your shop, the gun's shooter could be put in harm's way.

TIPS ON CHOKE TUBES

Applying oil to the threads before screwing in a choke tube makes it much easier to remove. Shooters should also be sure that a choke tube is screwed in as tightly as possible, checking after each volley of shots to avoid barrel damage.

Ported barrels get dirty very fast. And a ported barrel or choke tube clogged with debris quickly loses its effectiveness.

The interior ballistics of steel-shot loads account for why steel leaves behind so much carbon residue in the barrel, particularly in the choke tube. There are shotgun and choke-tube cleaners now available that are specifically formulated to combat this problem.

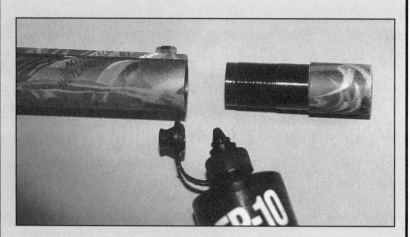

The threads of a screw-in choke tube should always be lubed before installation.

Chapter 6

THE STOCK

There is something sensual about the feel and smell of a wooden gunstock against your cheek. Gunstocks have been carved from ivory, cast from metals, molded from polymers, and layered with fiberglass. But good old wood is, of course, the most common and successful medium for stock making. And a long list of woods have been used: birch and beech, oak and pine, ash, cherry, mesquite, myrtle, pecan, holly, teak, mahogany, madrone, persimmon, and I'm sure a few other native American woods that I've left out. African ekki, ebony, benge, bubinga, sifou, and other exotics have also been tried.

But there is a favorite. Walnut, in its many forms, reigns supreme as the base material for fabricating gunstocks. It is strong, durable, light, and flexible. It looks and smells good, is easy to work, and takes finishes well. American black walnut is indigenous to the eastern U.S., while Claro walnut, otherwise known as California or Hinds, is found in the West.

Walnut is so popular that you'll also find several foreign varieties growing on these shores, as well as hybrids. Treasured exotic walnuts include Circassian, Turkish, Persian, Himalayan, Bastogne, English, French, and Spanish — each with its own distinctive color and tone, grain and feather. But American black walnut is the densest and hardest of all. It is also stiffer and doesn't flex under recoil like European walnut does.

If a shotgun is a tool, the stock is its handle, the part with which the shooter makes the most intimate contact. It must be sturdy and comfortable, and of course it hurts nothing if it looks good.

Personal comfort and taste will dictate whether the shooter likes the looks and feel of a straight grip or pistol-style grip. Double guns, regardless of grade, will undoubtedly feature hand-cut and probably elaborate checkering (the higher the grade, the more elaborate) on the grip and forend, while an inexpensive gun in any other action usually comes with stamped checkering or none at all.

For a shooter who is used to a pistol grip, an English-style (straight) grip will put the thumb dangerously close to the nose

Replacement stocks are available in a wide variety of woods.

when the shotgun is mounted. A grip that is too thin will tend to dip the shooter's elbow on his grip hand, which actually pulls the barrel in that direction. A palm swell, cut, molded, or adhered to the grip, can correct this problem.

Regardless of how it looks and feels, however, the stock is still a handle. And that handle must fit the shooter or the gun is simply a tomato stake.

FITTING A RECOIL PAD

A recoil pad is added to the stock to lessen felt recoil. Many styles are available, but the most popular versions right now are made of Sorbothane, an energy-absorbing synthetic material first designed for pilot helmets, or have high-tech designs such as those produced by Sims Limbsaver and Tri-Viz, which use air-filled compartments that collapse at a measured rate, thus delaying recoil and spreading out its effect.

A sporting-clays shooter or bird hunter needs a pad that is rounded at the top so it doesn't catch on the shirt or jacket as the shotgun is mounted. Trap and skeet gunners start with the shotgun already mounted and prefer a curved pad that covers more of the shoulder, distributing the recoil over a larger area.

Turkey and deer hunters, who shoot magnum loads from mounted positions, need thicker recoil pads. Dove hunters, who usually shoot in light shirts, also need thicker versions; not as much to combat recoil as to compensate for the longer length of pull created by the lack of bulky clothing.

Regardless of the type of recoil pad you choose, fitting it to the stock requires just a few easy steps. First, don't use a carpenter's saw if you need to shorten the stock. You are better off with a very fine-toothed miter saw, using just enough force to cut the wood, but not so much that you splinter across the grain. Once you cut through the side of the stock top to bottom, turn it over and cut from the

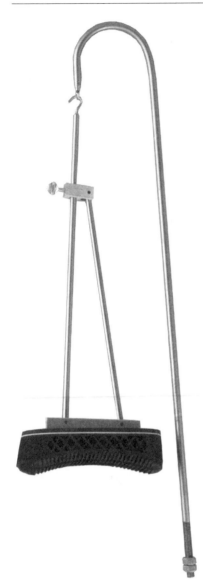

B&R recoil pad fitting jig.

other side. Wood is less likely to splinter if you cut into it rather than out of it, so don't cut completely through from one side to the other.

Fixing splintered edges is such a time-consuming, maddening task that it's definitely better to take precautions to avoid it as much as possible.

An even better choice is to cut the stock with a carbide blade in a radial-arm saw or table saw. High rpm and a slow feed rate are ideal for creating a clean edge with no chipping. Remember that if you shorten a stock it might change the pitch (the angle on the end of the stock), which can only be adjusted by making another angled cut.

It is, of course, imperative that the stock-shortening cut, and any subsequent adjustments, be made at a right angle to the line of the stock. The best way to ensure that this cut is made safely and correctly on a table saw is to secure the stock in a special cradle (available through Brownells). Seal the newly exposed wood to keep moisture from seeping under the new pad and into the stock.

If you shorten a stock by more than ⅜ inch, the old screw holes won't orient with the new pad. Sometimes the old heel screw hole will be at a different angle but still useable, but don't expect the toe screw hole to be useful at all.

Putting the stock in a recoil pad jig makes the job easier, although you may prefer the freedom of movement you get by holding it in your hands. B-Square and Miles Gilbert made good jigs.

Use the template from the new pad (or the pad itself) to mark the new hole locations. If they are too close to the old holes (closer than the diameter of a hole), drill out the old holes with a quarter-inch drill and plug them with a hardware store dowel cut to size. Or simply fill the hole with AcraGlass bedding epoxy or something equivalent and let it dry.

Some pads won't have screw holes cut in the surface. Turn them over and insert a punch in the screw hole indent on the inside face and push until it makes a dent on the outside of the pad. Using a soaped (dishwashing soap) razor blade, slice down until you contact the punch point. Remove the blade, soap it again, and make a second cut perpendicular to the first (crossing it in an X-pattern).

Now soap the screw threads and press the screw through. I like to put a little soap on the part of the screwdriver tip that will actually enter the pad material and turn the screws into the stock holes. Don't substitute oil, Vaseline, or a petroleum-based lubricant for the dishwashing soap, or you may stain the pad material. Once the screwdriver is removed, the screw holes should disappear.

Now the pad must be trimmed. Always buy a pad that is slightly larger than the depth of your stock. Use care when trimming because if you remove too much of the perimeter from some high-tech pads, it compromises the effectiveness of the pad.

Place three layers of masking tape on the stock finish, flush with the pad, and draw a pattern on the top layer of tape. Use a belt or disk sander (with safety glasses, hearing protection, a

When installing a new recoil pad, soap up a razor blade and cut slots for the holding screws to pass through.

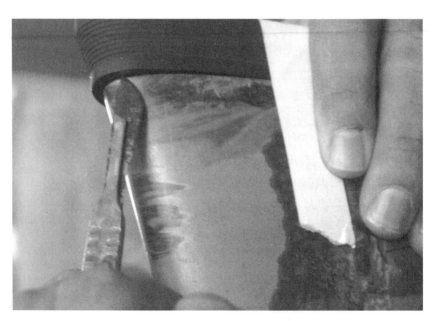

Attach the pad and scribe the outline of the stock on the face of the pad.

With the pad on the jig, sand it down to the scribe marks, being careful to keep the face of the pad at a right angle to the sanding surface.

When the pad is sanded roughly to the marked dimension, remove it from the jig and attach it to the stock again. Cover the end of the stock with several layers of masking tape to protect the finish during final sanding, removing and re-marking the tape as sanding progresses.

breathing mask, and good light) to grind the pad until the pattern disappears on the tape. Now mark the next layer and grind until that disappears. Repeat with the third layer, using a very light touch and being careful not to knick the stock's finish.

When you finish sanding down the sides, place tape along the heel and toe and grind them as well, blending to the curve of the sides. Final finish work can be done with an extremely fine file, applied lightly and sparingly.

STOCK WORK

For a variety of reasons, stock work on shotguns is rare these days for anyone but specialists. Fixing a dinged or cracked stock often takes more time than it's worth, particularly when it can simply be replaced with one of the abundant and affordable wood or synthetic alternatives.

The stock on most shotguns, regardless of action, is removed by inserting a socket wrench or long screwdriver into the buttstock to unscrew the fastening rod.

If you want to fix a split stock just for the experience, or to repair a stock that can't be replaced eas-  *Brownells' stock takedown set.*
ily, it can certainly be
done. The best way is to pry open the crack, work in a small amount of epoxy, and clamp it shut. If clamping the curved surface of the stock proves difficult, you can drill holes for brass pins (which are epoxied in place) and then file them down smooth. This provides more strength if you're working with a piece that has been broken completely off the stock. Brownells sells kits for this very purpose.

If the stock on an expensive or rare gun is damaged, the owner will likely take it to someone with a great deal of experience. My gunsmithing friend Rick Hammond gets a lot of work from people looking to re-stock or repair the woodwork on old doubles. Guns come to his tiny shop from all over the country because such work is beyond the skills of most gunsmiths.

Nevertheless, virtually anyone interested in gunsmithing has at one time or another wanted to "custom stock" a gun. And, regardless of the results of these attempts, we should all have a basic knowledge of what is involved in repairing and refinishing shotgun stocks.

Maybe it's because I deal mostly with hunting guns—shooting tools used by folks who expect to pick up a few dings and dents—but I just can't see the value of fixing blemishes on stocks.

But it can be done, and here's how.

Let's start with raising dents, which should be part of any Gunsmithing 101 class. Fixing a dent is the only stock repair most average gunsmiths are willing to make these days. A dent is actually just a depression in the fibers of the wood, and simply expanding the fibers solves the problem.

To raise a dent, gather a soldering iron, an old towel, and a cup of water. Soak a corner of the towel in water and place the wet part over the dent, being careful not to wet the area surrounding the dent. Now place the soldering iron on the towel directly over the dent. The heat will turn the water to steam, which in turn will be directed into the compressed wood fibers, expanding them.

Don't hold the iron on the towel too long, or it will scorch the wood finish. As long as you see steam coming from the towel, you're all right.

Repeat the procedure until the dent is fully raised. It may take three applications or it may take twenty, depending on the depth of the dent, the type of wood, and the finish.

This simple procedure should repair about 90 percent of the dents you encounter. The other 10 percent, usually larger and deeper dents, may require a little more attention and a slightly different application of the same procedure.

You'll need a sealable, heatable can or jar with a top into which a 2-inch piece of ⅛-inch copper tubing can be inserted and soldered in place. Hook a foot-long piece of rubber tubing over it and insert another 2-inch piece of the same copper tubing in the other end to serve as a nozzle.

With water in the can or jar, place it on a heat source to boil, which will force steam down the hose. Use the hose to apply a steady stream of steam directly to the center of the dent for a minute or two and watch it heal.

This procedure will not repair a gouge where wood has actually been removed from the stock. These must be filled with a wood filler like a shellac stick or wood dust and glue of the correct color, or by splicing in an inlay. But achieving an exact match with any of these methods is extremely difficult.

Splits and cracks along the grain can be repaired by drilling, epoxying, and pinning the pieces together. Tape, clamps, or straps can be used to hold everything tightly in place until the epoxy dries. Brownells sells stock pins of varying lengths for just this application.

It's not unusual to see the toe broken off a shotgun stock that's fallen off a truck tailgate or out of a treestand. If the toe can be recovered and/or reshaped to fit, it can be drilled, epoxied, and pinned back in place. But if you have to replace the piece, it will require intricate shaping and fitting and finishing for a piece of wood that probably isn't going to match very well. Unless the gun is obsolete, you're probably better off just buying a replacement stock.

Many damaged shotgun forends are even more of a hassle to repair—and just as easy to replace. It's certainly possible to fix them, but their shape and size make the job difficult.

Making your own stock falls more in the realm of gunmakers than gunsmiths. It's a highly specialized skill. In the most sophisticated shops, templates of existing stocks and forends can be made with computerized wood-shaping equipment, but it's not cheap.

REFINISHING

Virtually every gunsmith will need to refinish a stock at some point, particularly if he does any shaping or alterations to accommodate gunfit. If you rasp off a section of comb or toe or reshape a grip, you're going to have to know how to refinish the stock so that the whole thing matches.

Old finish can be removed with a chemical or electric stripper and/or sanding, after which dents and blemishes must be addressed before it can be refinished. But there is a process available that scrubs off the old finish and uses heat to fix any dents at the same time.

You'll need a bucket of hot water mixed with a half-cup of bleach and a half-cup of Mr. Clean cleaner. Wear rubber gloves and apply the solution to the stock with a scrub brush. Rub for about five minutes, wipe the suds off with a cloth, and then hold the stock over a heat source to dry the wood.

Obviously, you don't want to scorch the wood, just heat it enough to raise the grain. When you can't see any more moisture on the wood, rub the entire stock with 2/0 steel wool to clean off the "whisker" and remove more of the finish. Repeat the entire procedure until all signs of the old finish are gone.

This process should raise most dents in the wood while the finish is being removed. Stubborn dents can be raised with a direct application of heat as discussed earlier in this chapter. Many stocks will be ready for a final sanding after three or four applications of the solution and heat. Others, however, may require fifteen or twenty applications. Concentrate on stubborn spots. If the applications don't bring out all of the oil, mix a little plain paint whiting and a grease solvent and brush this on the trouble spot. Heat the spot, and when oil comes out, wipe it away and treat the area with the whiting solution.

When all of the old finish is removed, sand the stock completely, starting with a medium grade and working to very fine, then polish the wood with fine (4/0) steel wool. Now clean the entire stock with an application of turpentine and allow it to dry.

There are a host of commercial finishes available—Dem-Bart and Birchwood Casey have complete lines—including polyurethane and epoxy, but probably the best all-around finish for novices and professionals alike is linseed oil with fast-drying additives.

CHECKERING

Checkering is the process of cutting diamond-shaped patterns on the trips and forearms of shotguns to enhance aesthetics and the shooter's grip. The work is intricate, slow, and painstaking, and

A jig is a virtual necessity when checkering a shotgun stock.

definitely not for everyone. That's the reason mass-produced commercial shotguns use stamped checkering.

Checkering is another procedure that all gunsmiths should be familiar with, but that only a few talented artisans will attempt to tackle. Still, virtually anyone who tries his hand at gunsmithing will attempt a checkering job at some point.

Three basic styles of checkering dominate the field—American, English, and French—with some variations of each. Checkering requires special cutting tools with very sharp blades, and the process is aided greatly by using a special cradle to hold the piece and commercial paper decal patterns to follow.

Complete checkering kits, with the required V, border, and spacing cutting gouges in single-line, 2-, 3-, 4- and skip-line, and bend configurations, are available for twenty dollars and up. Commercial cradles run around thirty dollars. Power checkering tools are also available.

Paper patterns can be purchased through gunsmithing supply houses. They are cut out and affixed to the stock, and the initial guidelines are cut through the pattern and into the wood with a V-tool or sharp knife.

Most patterns are generally cut at fourteen to twenty-four lines per inch with eighteen- to twenty-liners a good starting point. Single-line cutters come in a variety of degrees, which are used according to the hardness of the stock wood. Coarse patterns provide a better grip, but fine patterns offer better aesthetics. You'll likely develop a personal preference if you are serious enough to tackle the project.

Practice before you start gouging a gunstock—first on a flat piece of hardwood, then on an old baseball bat (to get practice on a curved object), then maybe on a throwaway gunstock. Believe me, checkering takes a lot of practice. You'll need to get the feel of each cutter and each type of cut to determine the degree

Checkering requires specialty tools, a good pattern, and a lot of practice.

of care required to achieve uniformity in depth and spacing. Once a cut is made it's there to stay; there is no eraser.

Use a straightedge to make a simple straight line. Then score the line using a single-line cutting tool. Next, use a double-line tool to make a series of parallel lines, all with a back-and-forth cutting motion. During practice you should experiment with the vertical angle of the cutter. The more vertical the shaft, the deeper the point will cut; the lower the angle, the shallower—and of course the depth and resistance will vary with the hardness of the particular wood being cut, which is why it helps to do a final practice run on wood as similar as possible to the actual stock.

If you are artistic and meticulous and want to produce fine gunstocks, perhaps checkering will appeal to you. If you're production- or service-minded and always looking to get started on the next job, you'll probably leave checkering to those select few specialists who do it well.

Chapter 7

―――

GUNFIT

A nyone involved in gunsmithing needs to know the basics of gunfit. And with the aptitude and knowledge to do stock modifications, fitting can be a major part of a gunsmith's business.

Regardless of your choice of guns, you will likely shoot it better if you shoot it comfortably. This is because your dominant eye actually serves as the rear sight on a shotgun. How it aligns with the barrel (not necessarily the front bead, which should be ignored when wingshooting) dictates where the gun will shoot.

This positioning must be exactly the same every time for consistent results. An ⅛-inch difference in the positioning of your cheek on the stock moves the point of impact more than a foot at forty yards.

The vast majority of American shooters just buy guns off the rack and adjust their shooting style to fit—physical contortions are often necessary to place cheek on stock or front hand on forend to make the gun "fit" the shooter.

Europeans, on the other hand, feel that it is imperative that the gun be fit to the shooter. That is, the gun must have the proper

All gunsmiths should have a basic understanding of gunfit.

drop and cast to the stock so that it points exactly where the shooter is looking as soon as it's mounted. In Europe, gun ownership is a privilege afforded to a small minority of the population—folks with money who can afford to follow tradition and pay to have guns custom fitted to their physiques. There simply aren't many Wal-Mart Mossbergs available in Europe.

So a gun bought off a dealer's shelf is a compromise. It probably fits no one perfectly, but can be used casually by virtually anyone. But good fit makes a gun far more efficient, particularly in the hands of someone who already knows how to shoot.

Professional fitting, which is the best option if the shooter is serious about wingshooting with a particular gun, is usually only available at custom shops, wingshooting schools, or high-end dealers that have the resources and training to tailor every aspect of the gun to fit you. Customers can expect to pay at least two hundred dollars for a fitting, particularly if it includes shooting a "try gun" (adjustable for pitch, length, cast, and so on) at a range.

THE ELEMENTS OF GUNFIT

Critical stock measurements in fitting a gun to a particular shooter include length of pull, drop, pitch, and cast. But let's start with the most common bugaboo, length of pull. Pull is the distance from the front of the trigger shoe (or the front trigger on a double-trigger gun) to the center of the buttstock.

Most factory guns come out of the box with a length of pull at 14 to 14⅜ inches. If your sleeve length is thirty-two inches and you commonly shoot in light clothing, this should be a decent fit. But not everyone fits that criterion. Youth or ladies'

Measuring length of pull.

models, for example, often come with a length of pull in the 12-to 12½-inch range.

If the stock is too short, your gun will shoot high. Also, you'll probably bang your nose with the thumb of your trigger hand, which will make you move your hand around looking for a comfortable spot on the stock. Conversely, if the pull is too long the gun will shoot low, make mounting difficult, and be a real bear when you're chasing fast crossing targets.

Most of us simply adjust to the length of pull on our specific guns. Creeping the lead hand farther forward on the forend is a method used to artificially lengthen a gun that is slightly short.

So just shorten or lengthen the stock, right? Yes, but then you've changed the comb (the top of the stock where your cheek rests) height, since shotgun stocks typically slope downward toward the butt. And if you remove more than a quarter-inch from the end of the stock you're going to need another recoil pad because the old one will be too small.

A gun can be lengthened by adding spacers or a thicker recoil pad. If you have to add wood, it's difficult to match grain and most likely will necessitate staining and refinishing the entire stock to hide the differences. It's much easier to simply replace the stock with a longer one.

Synthetic stocks are hollow, which leaves you with few, if any, alteration options. For instance, since there is nothing in the center of the butt of a synthetic stock to which you can affix a recoil pad, it is fastened by screws to threaded metal inserts in the plastic. Shorten the stock and you cut off the inserts. I've seen some attempts at filling the recess in shortened synthetic stocks to give the recoil-pad screws purchase, but I'm not sure they were worth the effort.

Factory field guns usually come at 1½ inches of drop comb height, trap guns about ⅛ inch less. Thus, the comb also must be adjusted whenever the pull is altered.

You can add lift with a strap-on or stick-on pad or moleskin, and cast can be added the same way. Remember, ¹⁄₁₆ inch moves the point of aim an inch at fifteen yards, and ⅛ inch moves it a foot at forty yards.

Drop is the measurement taken at the topmost surface of a shotgun's stock that determines the elevation of the shooter's head and eye in relation to the bore. To measure drop, a straightedge is laid upon the rib or on top of the barrels and a measurement taken from the bottom of the straightedge to the top of the stock.

Drop at the comb is measured at the very front top of the comb. Drop at the face is an optional measurement taken midway

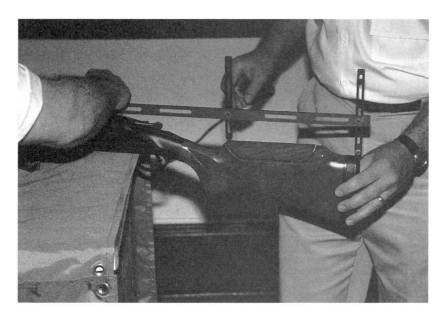

Measuring drop at the comb and heel.

between the front, top surface of the comb and the heel. This is the point at which the shooter's face contacts the stock. Because of variations in exact placement, drop at the face is not often thought of as a major factor in gunfitting.

Drop at the heel is measured at the farthest end of the butt-stock, where the butt plate or recoil pad meets the top of the comb. It is a vital measurement in determining the placement of the shooter's head and eye on the gunstock.

Once those factors are adjusted you can fine-tune the fit by changing the gun's pitch, which is the angle the stock is cut to meet the shoulder. Normal, or down, pitch is considered 2 to 2½ inches.

Pitch governs how the butt fits against the shoulder. Too little pitch will allow the toe of the stock to dig into the shoulder and also has a tendency to allow the stock to slide down and off the shoulder when fired. Too much pitch, on the other hand, makes the stock slip up into the cheek, accentuating felt recoil.

Increasing the down pitch can help heavy men and well-endowed women by making the gun easier to mount and more comfortable. Decreasing the

Measuring pitch.

pitch makes it easier to hit fast-rising birds and reduces muzzle jump.

Careful gunfitting includes studying the shape of the shooter's shoulder and chest and adjusting the pitch to keep the gun comfortably in position. Women often require more pitch than men.

The most common way of measuring pitch is by standing the gunbutt on the floor with the action or receiver against a squared door frame, then noting the distance (amount of pitch) from the top of the rib to the vertical doorjamb. If the muzzle and barrel are flush to the wall in this position, it's called neutral pitch. If the muzzle touches the wall with the butt squarely on the floor and the receiver is not touching, it's negative pitch. Obviously, negative pitch is very difficult to measure.

The British method of fitting entails also taking measurements from the trigger to the toe, center, and heel of the stock, providing precise figures to use for proper adjustment of pitch.

You can also get into cast-on and cast-off if you're the type who has an affinity for absolute custom fit. Cast is a lateral bend in a buttstock that compensates for the thickness of the shooter's face. Cast-off is for right-handed shooters, cast-on for lefties.

If there is no cast in the original stock of your gun, it can be added by removing wood from the cheek side of the comb or having the stock bent with heat and a bending jig. Be advised that this is a job for an experienced professional. And they are paid well for that expertise.

Of course, we are not all experienced gunfit professionals, but then all shooters don't have the means to purchase the services of experienced pros, either. That's why Brownells sells kits

Graco adjustable butt plate.

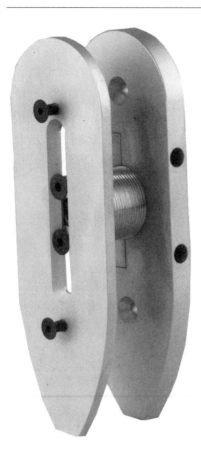

Graco adjustable comb hardware.

that can be installed on existing stocks (with some alteration) so that length of pull, cast, pitch, and comb height can be adjusted by mechanical means.

BIRTH OF A TRAP GUN

Trap- and sporting-clays shooters usually need the most fine-tuning for gunfit. When I first got into trapshooting I had no dedicated gun. After shooting several shotguns of varying proportions, however, I soon realized the value of proper gunfit. Being blessed with a rack of Ithaca M37s, I purchased a 30-inch trap barrel from the factory, put it on my turkey gun receiver, and added the honed-down trigger assembly from my DeerSlayer II.

The gun shot too flat with the conventional M37 stock, so I substituted a Monte Carlo version from another DeerSlayer II. It chased rising targets well but still needed a moleskin pad to get sufficient height. But now it tended to shoot to the right, partly because of the cast added by the moleskin overlapping down the cheek side of the stock. Rasping a tad off the cheek-piece gave my eye better alignment and moved the pattern back to the left.

I wanted to change to a softer recoil pad and chose a Sims, which was ⅜ inch thicker than the old one, changing the once-perfect length of pull. I trimmed the stock by ⅜ inch, which also changed the pitch slightly, necessitating another angled cut before the new pad could be attached.

The gun, known as Ole Paint by my trapfield compatriots due to the camo paint left over from its turkey-hunting days, has served me well. I found out that a personal weight gain of twenty pounds throws the point of aim to the left due to my chubbier cheeks, but when I do my dinner table push-aways the adjusted gun points like a laser.

Trap guns feature a raised rib, which makes the gun shoot high.

Women trap- and clays shooters often need cast in a stock to fit their face and additional cast at the toe to move it away from the breast. The top cast can be accomplished by adding a pad or trimming wood rather than bending the stock, but the heel cast must be done by a bender.

BALANCE IS IMPORTANT

Ideally, 50 percent of the gun's weight is between the hands, 25 in the buttstock, and 25 in the barrels. Shotguns for target shooting, however, have more forward weight, which tends to steady the hold and accentuate the barrel swing.

A gun that fits well is beneficial to trapshooters and wingshooters, but it doesn't mean much if you're hunting turkeys, shooting waterfowl over decoys, or shooting a slug gun, where a quick gun mount isn't critical to success.

CHECKING THE FIT

When a shotgun fits, you should be able to mount it with your eyes closed and find the rib or bead perfectly aligned when you open them. It's helpful to take this one step further with a trip to the shooting range to see where the shot charge centers in relation to a pre-marked aiming point.

Set up a pattern board at sixteen yards, focus on a marked aiming point, shoulder the gun quickly but smoothly, and fire. A

After ensuring the gun is empty, a professional gunfitter can look down the rib while the gun is mounted to determine if cast, pitch, and drop need to be altered.

trend should emerge from that pattern, assuming you didn't jerk or pull at the shot. Measuring from the center of the aiming point, each inch of displacement translates to a stock adjustment of ⅟₁₆ inch. (I'm told that it's a tenet of the Churchill method of shooting.)

If the comb of your gun is too high, you'll center your pattern too high. If it's too low, your eye is too low, and the pattern will obviously be low. A shooter with a pudgy face will generally shoot higher with a particular gun than a thin-faced shooter with the same gun, because the mass of the "fuller" face puts the eye in a higher position.

If you're shooting to the left or right, the cast may need an adjustment to bring your eyes in line with the barrel.

Chapter 8

PATTERNING

Once the shot charge leaves the barrel it spreads to varying degrees, depending on the choke, barrel configuration, distance, and type and size of the pellet. The manner in which it spreads is your pattern. Your shotgun's pattern is its signature. How that particular barrel and choke combination throws a specific load at a specific distance is a dynamic and variable feature unique to that gun. Change chokes or loads and the pattern changes.

Patterning techniques vary with the gun's application. Turkey hunters need an extremely full-choked, dense pattern that will be fired from a stationary barrel aimed like a rifle at a standing bird's head and neck. Wingshooters, on the other hand, need to quickly throw consistent, wide, and well-distributed patterns at varying distances to nail flying targets.

A common misconception among shotgunners is that a larger gauge throws a larger pattern. After all, it's easier to score in skeet or trap with a 12-gauge than with a 20. But while it's easier to break birds with the larger gauge, that is not because of the size of the pattern.

The rate of shot spread is controlled by the choke and other factors, not by the bore diameter. Theoretically, the pattern is about the same size whether it comes from a 12-, 16-, 20-, or 28-gauge. In actual use, you'll probably score higher and find the pattern marginally wider with the big bore because there are more pellets in the shot string and more will be deformed and/or pressured outward. This swells the pattern diameter a bit, but it doesn't really make a difference in the size of the pattern.

At 15 yards a shooter with a full-choke gun can count on a pattern with a 12-inch diameter—or 16 inches from a modified barrel—regardless of gauge. At 25 yards, the full choke patterns about 24 inches in diameter and the modified 28 inches, again without regard to gauge.

POINT OF IMPACT

Most modern raised-rib shotguns, no matter what type of action they have, center their patterns a bit high, usually 4 to 8 inches above the line of sight at 40 yards. Trap guns are aligned to print 6 to 12 inches high at that distance because the trap targets are always rising.

Exceptions to this would be pumps, bolts, and autoloaders designed for turkey and deer hunting. Since these guns are designed to be aimed rather than pointed, their stocks and sight systems are configured to allow them to shoot straight-on.

Side-by-side doubles have more flexible barrels and often throw their patterns a bit low. But don't take that as gospel without checking it at the range. Winchester regulated its classic Model 21 to shoot slightly low, but in 1960, for reasons that stayed in the boardroom, it changed its mind and moved the point of impact to dead-on. Over-unders usually shoot slightly higher because the effect of gravity stiffens the barrels, which sit one on top of the other.

Success in the field begins with patterning at the shooting range.

TO THE PATTERNING BOARD

It is essential to test a shotgun on a patterning board with the types of loads that will be used in the field. Some clubs use a whitewashed steel or iron plate for this. Lead pellets hitting the surface leave distinctive marks that can be "erased" by rolling another layer of paint over the pattern, ready for the next shot. This type of board should only be used with soft lead shot, however, as steel and other hard shot can ricochet.

Any safe backdrop that will accommodate a 40-square-inch sheet of paper (two strips of wide butcher paper taped together work fine) will do as a patterning board. In fact, this set-up is more useful than the steel plate because pellet counts can be determined away from the range, where shot-to-shot comparisons can be made.

A waterfowl hunter's shotgun won't pattern the same as a turkey hunter's because the guns are used differently.

I like to pattern new guns with an initial shot from a solid rest on a bench at fifteen yards to determine if the gun shoots where it is aimed. This only tells you the alignment of the barrel-choke partnership. Follow that with an offhand shot from the same distance, since the gun will likely shoot to a different point of aim from your shoulder than from the bench.

Most "bespoke" (custom-made guns, usually doubles) still use fixed chokes. A highly experienced barrel borer regulates them to a specific shot size, weight, and velocity. A Wal-Mart 870 pump is built to less stringent standards and will accept a wider variety of loads, printing some well and others not so well. Today's production guns, particularly less expensive models, don't always shoot straight.

Once you've determined where your gun shoots, examine *how* it shoots. The industry standard is a target set at 40 yards with a 30-inch circle at the center. The number of pellets your pattern throws within the circle determines the efficiency percentage of your pattern. For example, an 80-percent pattern means that 8 out of every 10 pellets in that particular load fell within that circle at that distance.

The industry standard pattern percentage at that distance is 60 to 70 percent for a full choke; 55 to 60 percent for modified; and 45 percent (in an optimum load) for improved-cylinder.

You'll find that different load and pellet sizes will pattern differently out of the same choke. It all has to do with the dynamics of barrel and choke. When patterning a gun and load, don't base your judgment on one or two shots. You'll need at least ten shots to get an approximate idea of where and how a gun is patterning.

A 30-inch circle at 40 yards is the industry standard for determining the "percentage" of a choke's efficiency.

In fact, various industry experts have told me that it takes at least one hundred patterns to get an accurate assessment (more than 95 percent surety) of a particular gun/load combination. For general use, however, few of us need that kind of efficiency—or the shoulder bruising and expense.

There are, believe it or not, scientific methods of thorough pattern reading. I know of only a couple of shooters sufficiently obsessed to utilize such means in patterning their guns. Oh, they are good shooters; very good, in fact, but strange people. I've heard of methods like the Berlin-Wanasse and Thompson-Oberfell, but I have never tried them because there are far less elaborate ways to determine the efficiency of your pattern.

The late Don Zutz used to preach the importance of the "annular ring," a donut drawn around the core but inside the confines of the 30-inch circle. First, understand that experts look

Because turkey guns pattern so tightly, it is essential to know the size of the pattern at different distances.

for two different pellet distributions in any pattern: the core or center of the dispersion (usually 20 inches in diameter) and the annular ring (a 5-inch-wide strip surrounding the core).

Why is the annular ring so important? Even the best shots aren't going to center every target, and having sufficient pellets consistently in the annular ring simply expands your efficiency and margin of error.

Not all chokes and loads are efficient at the "useable" fringes of the pattern, even if they throw a dense core pattern. The tendency toward high core density is increased by such things as harder (high-antimony) lead shot that withstands pellet-deforming setback pressures; copper or nickel-plated shot; or steel, tungsten, and other exotics. This occurs because the sturdier pellets remain round, flying straighter to the core of the target. Even open-bored chokes, cylinder-bore, skeet, and improved-cylinder can hammer the core with hard pellets without filling in the annular ring very well.

To be efficient, a pattern must spread sufficiently into that annular ring. The standard 30-inch circle at 40 yards is not always the most practical way to assess a pattern. It's better to determine the average shooting range for the game being pursued

There is no need to scribe annular rings on a turkey patterning board; the important pellet count is at the core of the pattern.

and then test over that distance. A trapshooter, for instance, wants to pattern at 32 to 35 yards for 16-yard events and at 40 yards for optimum handicap distances.

Skeet shooters are better off patterning at 17 to 20 yards because most shoot their birds before they reach the NSSA distance of 21 yards at midfield. For hunters, the average shot at woodcock or quail may be 15 yards and 25 yards for pheasants, but a goose or turkey hunter may want to know his pattern at 50 yards.

Patterning at a specified distance tells you much more than the 30-inch, 40-yard standard. Shoot at a specified aiming point,

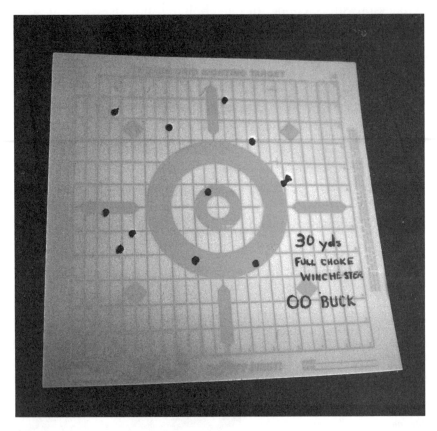

Buckshot patterns deteriorate quickly with distance.

but don't draw the circles until after the shot. Then draw the appropriate circles around the area of greatest density. It helps to do it this way because shotguns are not accurate enough to center their patterns in pre-drawn circles.

Again, the point of emphasis is that annular ring. Your goal should be to find the load that puts the most pellets in that ring and spreads them most consistently over the area.

How many pellets is enough? It depends on whom you ask. But Don Zutz's estimation was that three pellets were needed in every area of the target that could be covered with a clay bird, since they are about the size of the vital area of most gamebirds. More is better, but three pellets should be sufficient.

Chapter 9

DEALING WITH RECOIL

There is probably nothing that discourages enthusiasm for shotgun shooting faster than the ravages of recoil. Shotguns kick. It's simply the nature of the beast—an accepted facet of the instrument and the exercise. But how much abuse the shooter has to accept is controllable.

Isaac Newton warned the world long ago that for every action there will be an equal and opposite reaction. That's pretty much the definition of shotgun recoil: Trip that trigger and there will be punishment at both ends.

You can lessen recoil by changing loads, going to a smaller gauge or heavier gun, or using a gas-operated autoloader instead of a double or pump.

You'll find that it's not just novices and wimps who'd like to soften recoil. In fact, the desire to soften recoil isn't always about black and blue. A 12-gauge trap or sporting-clays gun, for example, isn't really a hard-kicking beast, but anything that can soften the cumulative effect of one hundred shots fired in a short period of time is certainly welcome. Recoil reduction is also an aid in maintaining concentration, which can lead to better shooting.

That's the reason we're seeing more and more 1-ounce 12-gauge loads on trapfields and even ⅞-ounce international loads in the shellbags of sporting-clays competitors. The lighter loads recoil less and actually pattern better, effectively eliminating the extra pellets that are wasted at the periphery of the patterns of larger loads.

Shotguns that shoot slugs, buckshot, turkey, or waterfowl loads, however, all mete out considerable punishment every time the trigger is pulled. Stuffed with heavy loads, these guns can recoil with more energy than elephant loads in big rifles.

And it's not just the kick. It's the perception created by the kick, sound, and barrel jump that adds up to "perceived recoil," which is really what we're dealing with.

A gunsmith has several recoil-reducing options he can try. The perception can be reduced by lengthening forcing cones, even backboring barrels and/or porting barrels. I've noted elsewhere in this book that these particular modifications do little to

The shoulders of turkey and deer hunters take quite a pounding from today's powerful loads.

change the physics of actual recoil, but they can make the perception softer.

Just remember that while porting the barrel reduces barrel jump, which keeps the shooter on the target better and lessens perceived recoil, it also makes the report much louder. If the gun will be used for clay-target shooting, where hearing protection is always required, porting may be an asset. But if you port a hunting gun, the shooter's unprotected ears may convince him or her that recoil is actually greater. Fortunately, shooting at live targets draws the hunter's focus away from recoil.

THE GUN MUST FIT THE SHOOTER

One big step in controlling recoil is to make sure that the firearm fits the user. Generally speaking, novice shooters will be youngsters or women. Again speaking generally, they will be smaller-framed than the average adult male for whom almost all firearms are designed.

A small-framed person needs a smaller gun—one that is as user-friendly as possible. Shooting a gun that doesn't fit will result in much heavier felt recoil.

Virtually every manufacturer now makes a shorter-stocked, thinner-gripped "youth" or even "ladies" model, usually in 20-gauge. These guns feature the same receivers, actions, and barrels as the conventional versions of the same model, so a smaller stock can be replaced with a "real" one if the shooter outgrows the smaller version or the gun changes hands.

By the same token, a conventional shotgun can be fitted to smaller-framed shooters with stock and forearm kits from the aftermarket. Outers and other manufacturers offer youth or ladies kits, although most aftermarket kits are typically limited to Remington 870, 1100, and sometimes 11–87s, and, in lesser numbers, to Winchester 1300s, Mossberg 500s, and occasionally the Ithaca M37.

It's the ultimate folly to start a novice off with a heavy, bigbore gun and "let them grow into it." When teaching a youngster to drive you don't put the driver's seat back too far for them to reach the pedals and steering wheel in the hope that they will "grow into it."

Smaller people need smaller shotguns. But beware of that statement. If a gun has a lot of drop in the comb of the stock, the sensation of recoil will be even greater. Fitting squarely into that category are "youth" 20-gauge single-shot guns regrettably chambered for 3-inch loads. They may feel light to carry, but that joy does an immediate about-face when the trigger is pulled.

The economically priced, lightweight single shots are built to sell, not to shoot, and the recoil they dole out can go a long way toward discouraging a new shooter.

Granted, smaller shooters do need shotguns with less weight for their smaller arms; something with a shorter stock that keeps the center of gravity to the rear and affords a comfortable reach to the trigger. But don't think that just cutting off the buttstock will solve everything. For one thing, just sawing off the stock will change the gun's pitch, which could actually accentuate recoil.

The grip and forearm size is as important as stock length when fitting a small-statured shooter. A large grip in small hands doesn't allow sufficient thumb-over placement, stretches the hand to reach the trigger, and accentuates felt recoil.

Pump shotguns are often chosen as starting guns because they are light, inexpensive, simple to use, and durable. But they also kick hard. My daughter (the engineer) says that it's all explained by Thorson's Restatement of the Second Law of Thermodynamics. In layman's terms Thorson said "you can't get something for nothing."

The physical reaction (backward thrust) when a specific load explodes in a chamber always exerts the same amount of energy backward. A heavier gun, however, slows down that reaction, reducing recoil.

OTHER MODIFICATIONS

Another way to add weight while lessening recoil—without altering swing dynamics—is to install barrel tubes. For three or four hundred dollars you can have a set made for just about any double. The maker will need to know the make and model of the gun and the chokes for each barrel, and may even ask to have the barrels shipped to him for a better fit. Less expensive chamber inserts are available that serve the same purpose, using the existing barrel dimension and chokes for a smaller gauge.

I have a set of 28-gauge Briley Companion tubes that weigh as much as a loaded 12-gauge shell when inserted into the barrels of my 12-gauge Fabarms Gama over-under. This is a wonderful quail and skeet gun that has virtually no recoil due to the reduced payload and attendant weight of the 12-gauge frame, and it will kill feathered or clay birds just as well as a 12-gauge, provided I do my part in the shooting area.

Gun weight is part of the reason that my choice for breaking in new shooters is to start them with an autoloader. Load one shell at a time if you want to limit the novice's firepower but take advantage

A set of Briley Companion tubes allows this 12-gauge over-under to shoot 28-gauge ammunition.

of that action's recoil- or gas-operated system to greatly reduce recoil.

The reason autoloaders kick less than other actions is that in addition to being heavier, they are specifically designed to divert some of the energy generated by firing the cartridge into operating the shell ejection and rechambering process. The energy used to operate the action doesn't run rearward into the shooter's shoulder and cheek.

Yes, autoloaders cost more and weigh more. If you can get past the first, though, you can get around the second. The Remington 1100 Youth Model, which comes in 20-gauge, is as light as most pump guns, yet has the recoil-absorption inherent in most autoloaders.

Regardless of your choice of action, recoil can be further tamed in a couple of ways. An aftermarket recoil pad will likely be thicker and more efficient than the one that comes on most shotguns. There are many available, from Pachymar's fabled Decelerator to miracle material and design models from Kickeez, HiViz, and Sims, a company that has virtually revolutionized the concept of dampening vibration on bows with a rubberized product.

This company is introducing recoil pads with large collapsible air pockets built in that work on the same principle as airbags in vehicles. Sims recoil pads come fitted for specific guns or in sandable models, and they are more effective in softening recoil than anything else I've ever tried. They come on selected Ithaca and Remington shotguns. (See chapter 6 for instructions on installing a recoil pad.)

No matter how well a stock conforms to the shooter, if the comb is too low to allow comfortable cheek placement while looking over the bead or through the scope—and many shotgun combs are—a comb lift can be added economically. Leather,

The Cheek-eez pad from Kick-eez.

lace-on Monte Carlo pads are available through Cabela's and Brownells, as are form pads from Beartooth, which simply slide on, or others that adhere to the stock.

Recoil can also be reduced by installing mercury suppression cylinders, sometimes called "Dead Mules," in the buttstock or magazine of the gun. These effective items work on simple physics—a counterweight blunts the rearward rush of the gun during recoil and spreads out the "recoil experience" over a longer period of time. It's the same basic principle behind the gas cylinder in an autoloader. The cylinders, which cost forty to eighty dollars or so, are simply dropped into the gun's magazine

A recoil suppression device makes shooting more comfortable and may even improve accuracy.

(using up shell space, of course) or in the bolt hole in the butt. Some guns, like Beretta semiautos, have specific weights that replace the magazine cap and serve the same purpose without taking up magazine space or adding to the gun's butt weight.

I also install strap-on weights on barrels or magazines of target or "practical" competition guns, thereby reducing felt recoil and aiding barrel swing. I used to pour a bag of shot in the stock of my AR-15 to tame it for service rifle competition and have seen trapshooters give similar treatment to the stocks of their long-barreled shotguns.

But remember, if gun balance is an issue, such as in wing-shooting, adding weight up front or in back is going to screw up your shooting.

Chapter 10

SPECIALTY-APPLICATION SHOTGUNS

There are two special applications where shotguns are asked to perform in a manner other than scattering a load of pellets in an ever-widening cloud—hunting for deer and turkey, for which shotguns are equipped and aimed like rifles.

Nearly one-third of the nation's ten million whitetail hunters now go afield armed with shotguns, and this number is likely to increase as municipalities continue to opt for the short-range shotgun over the long-distance killing power of modern rifles. Eight states currently mandate that only shotguns (and muzzleloaders) may be used for deer, and another twelve similarly handicap at least 40 percent of their hunters.

Let's look at the specific features of good slug guns and turkey guns and how they can be made to perform better.

MAKING YOUR SLUG GUN SHOOT BETTER

How accurate are slug guns? With the right conditions, sub-1-inch groups at 100 yards have been achieved by expert shooters

Deer hunters are continually demanding better accuracy from their shotguns.

with custom guns and saboted slugs. In the everyday world, with commercial ordnance and weekend shooting sessions, you'll find that anything inside 5 inches at 100 yards is asking a lot of an out-of-the-box production slug gun. A slug gun and load that groups inside of 3 or 4 inches at 100 yards is a tack driver.

It's also important to realize that 100-yard target accuracy isn't essential for the average slug hunter. Most hunting shots are taken well inside 80 yards at vital areas nearly twice the diameter of a basketball, so a difference of an inch or two at 100 yards is moot.

Nevertheless, everyone wants guns that shoot well. The good news is that virtually any slug gun can be made to perform better. In fact, almost all of them can be substantially improved.

IT STARTS WITH THE BARREL

With a slug gun, the barrel is the first consideration in improving performance, as it's the soul of any firearm. If you use your smoothbore barrel for other types of hunting and shooting, you can improve its performance by simply adding a screw-in rifled choke tube.

Virtually every shotgun manufacturer now offers a rifled choke tube for its guns, and there are plenty of others on the aftermarket, with Hastings leading the industry. I have a signature model 5-inch choke tube that's sold through Walker's Game Ear.

One warning note: Don't try to shoot slugs through a barrel that is backbored. These barrels are too big for slug shooting, allowing the slug to tilt slightly as it travels down the barrel. Just imagine how a tilting slug reacts when it hits the rifling.

If the barrel is not backbored, however, a rifled choke tube allows you to use high-tech sabot slugs, which give you a longer effective range and better ballistic efficiency. Don't bother with sabots in a conventional smoothbore—super-expensive sabots are made to be spun by rifling and won't effectively shed their sleeves if they aren't spinning.

Although some rifled choke tubes shoot well out to 80 yards or so, common sense should tell you that imparting a spin of 40,000 rpm on a slug that has already reached peak velocity when it hits the rifling is a lot less effective than spinning it from the chamber.

The Mossberg Model 695 is a modern bolt-action shotgun.

Next, make sure the twist rate is right for your particular load. The latest research shows that a fast twist (1-in-25 or 1-in-28, available from Ithaca, Browning, Winchester, Benelli, Beretta, Franchi, or Marlin) stabilizes saboted ammunition best while 1-in-34 rates are the best compromise for sabots and short full-bore slugs. A slow twist like 1-in-36 is ideal if you're shooting only full-bore slugs. Most 20-gauge barrels have 1-in-24 to 1-in-28 twist.

PINNING A SLUG BARREL

Regardless of the slug barrel you choose, pinning it fast to the receiver will make it shoot more accurately. This is true for any barrel on any gun other than a bolt-action, single shot. Binding the barrel to the receiver will take a great deal of the accuracy-destroying vibration out of the system. (Drill a hole in the re-

Pinning the barrel will improve the accuracy of any slug gun that doesn't already have a fixed barrel.

ceiver and tap it for a hardened set screw long enough to bear on the barrel sleeve, essentially mating the barrel and receiver.)

Some guns will improve more than others when the barrel is pinned, depending on how tightly the barrel sleeve fits into the receiver to start with. But it really does benefit virtually any gun. I've seen pumps and autoloaders go from throwing "patterns" to tight "groups" with the treatment.

The next step in improving the performance of a slug gun is to lighten and stiffen the trigger. Even if your gun is a "buck special" with rifle sights and maybe even a rifled barrel, it's going to have the same receiver and internal and trigger mechanism as its counterpart designed for pellets.

Honing trigger sears is a job for veteran gunsmiths, because the amount of honing necessary for a particular trigger can only be determined with hands-on experience. The weight of the trigger pull can be measured with a spring-loaded specialty tool known as a trigger gauge. But this identifies the weight required to trip the trigger, not the creep.

The cost for professional trigger work varies wildly. I've seen it done for as little as twenty-five dollars, although I know

Lightening a trigger and eliminating creep may also improve accuracy.

some shops that won't touch trigger work for less than a hundred dollars. The design and complexity of the trigger mechanism and the shotgun's action will factor into the price. In general, it's much more difficult to adjust triggers on semiautomatics than it is on pumps.

A shotgun trigger is designed to be slapped, not squeezed like a rifle trigger. And insurance carriers for gun companies like to see substantial creep in triggers that are also set for a hearty slap. The fear is slam-fire on recoil, and manufacturers err on the side of caution. I don't care if you're strong enough to crush cue balls with your fist, nobody can wring full potential out of a firearm with an 8- to 10-pound trigger pull. In a perfect world, we'd have slug guns with crisp 3- to 3½-pound pulls, but even a 5- or 6-pounder isn't bad so long as there's no creep.

Hastings offers a readily adjustable drop-in trigger system for Remingtons, but most gunsmiths can take the trigger down. Some guns can be adjusted more than others—Remingtons, Ithacas, and Berettas are fairly adjustable, while Mossbergs and Winchesters are not.

Some gunsmiths won't work on triggers due to liability issues and/or because such an adjustment voids the gun's warranty. But a little bit of knowledge and experience is all that's needed to make a vast improvement in performance.

THE STOCK

With a few exceptions, you are going to find that slug guns have shotgun stocks, which are more suited to wingshooting than to sighting through a scope. Mossberg offers a unique adjustable-comb system on its Model 500 pump, but any stock can be brought to the correct cheek position with a strap-on Monte Carlo trap pad from Cabela's, a foam version from Beartooth, or a stick-on adjustment pad from Cheek-eez.

A high-lift comb like the one on this aftermarket Bell & Carlson stock allows the slug shooter to see through a scope without lifting his head.

You're going to find that many of the factors that need attention to make a slug gun shoot better are also things that trapshooters work with: reduced barrel jump, higher combed stocks, softer triggers, and so on.

In fact, my favorite trap gun has an Ithaca Model 37 receiver fitted with a 30-inch, vent-rib barrel, to which I added a honed-down trigger and Monte Carlo stock (fitted with a Sims recoil pad) from my DeerSlayer II slug gun.

CRYOGENIC TEMPERING—ANOTHER CURE FOR INACCURATE GUNS

Vibration is the enemy of accuracy or consistency in shotguns as much as it is in rifles. The vibration of the barrel due to the concussion and the pressure of the ejecta flying down the tube is known as harmonics, and it must be controlled if the shotgun is to shoot accurately and consistently.

The amount of vibration and the severity of the whip are fairly constant from shot to shot in a particular gun, but ammunition typically isn't. You'll find that slugs and shotshells commonly vary ten to fifty fps, shot to shot, which means that the projectile or shot charge is leaving the whipping barrel in a slightly different position. And with a different point of impact.

I've been able to tame barrel harmonics in several trap and slug guns, not to mention a couple of rifles and a balky muzzle-loader, by having the barrels and, in some cases the receivers, cryogenically treated. As a gunsmith, it's certainly a service worth offering to customers.

Cryogenic tempering—the deep freezing and deep reheating of metals—changes the molecular structure, making it harder, stiffer. In many cases it also makes the metal less porous, which aids in subsequent cleaning.

Cryogenics have long been used to temper tools, machine parts, and cutters, and more recently vehicle brakes, race-car components, golf clubs, softball bats, tennis rackets, and, yes, firearms barrels.

I'm not a metallurgist. But I know through personal application that cryogenic tempering has improved the performance of my guns and the guns of others. Certainly some guns are helped more than others, though. With my own guns the difference was negligible in some cases, and profound in others.

There is no visible difference in the metal after it has been cryogenized, and with no way to predict how much improvement you'll see in an individual gun, you'll find a lot of shotgunners who are skeptical of its benefits.

One friend of mine, who has a background in chemistry and metallurgy, was a scoffer. He was also an AA trapshooter who'd bought a new high-dollar gun that simply didn't shoot well, despite the fact that it had been cut to the exact dimensions of his old one. After three trips back to the factory, where he was basically told that there was nothing wrong with the gun, my friend reluctantly tried having the barrel cryogenically treated. He's right back to hundred-straights, and cryogenics has another new believer.

All firearms are produced with internal stresses. As the metal is bored, reamed, and machined, mechanical stresses are created. As forgings and castings cool, the differing rates of temperature change introduce residual stresses. Even heat-treating leaves thermal stresses behind.

Careful manufacturing, of course, results in barrels that shoot well, stresses and all. Cryogenic stress relief, however, can improve even the high-quality barrels by relieving internal stresses. It's those stresses, or weak spots, that cause barrels to twist and arc as they heat up from firing.

At the end of a typical 10-shot trapshooting string, pattern placement can shift 6 inches in some shotguns. With 25 shots, pattern placement can shift up to 12 inches—a 40 percent change. At a very affordable cost, a cryogenic company will take a barrel down to minus 300 degrees Fahrenheit, hold it at that temperature for a predetermined time, and then slowly bring it up through the cycle to approximately 300 degrees.

There are several cryogenic companies out there, and having a barrel worked on usually runs under a hundred dollars, although this may vary widely. I have 300-Below Cryogenic Tempering Services of Decatur, Illinois (www.300below.com) do my work. They tell me that their process permanently refines the grain structure of a barrel at the molecular level and produces a homogeneously stabilized barrel, whatever that is. They also say that carbon particles precipitate as carbides into a lattice structure and fill the microscopic voids. This creates a denser, smoother surface that reduces friction, heat, and wear.

All I know is that the cryogenic process took a couple of guns that had exasperated me and turned them into good shooters. To my way of thinking, cryogenics helps shotgun barrels even more than rifle barrels. There is a lot more whip in a shotgun barrel, and the shot charge or slug remains in the barrel a lot longer than a bullet does in a rifle, so it's more influenced by harmonics.

DRESSING UP THE HUNTING SHOTGUN

Today's turkey and waterfowl hunters know that camouflaging their guns is an absolute necessity. The best way to get the camo pattern you want is with a film-dipping process.

It's called Second Skin. Gunsmiths take in a shotgun, dismantle it, and degrease the parts that are to be finished, then ship it to the dipping outlet in Virginia. The results are impressive, and the process fascinating.

My introduction to the procedure took place in the early 1990s when shotgun manufacturers started advertising guns finished by a company named ColorWorks in popular commercial camouflage patterns from Realtree, Trebark, and Mossy Oak.

My battle-scarred Ithaca M87 pump was an excellent performer, but its quality was cloaked in a decidedly austere pattern that the Ithaca Gun Company of the late 1980s called its "Camoseal" camouflage design.

Good camouflage is now standard on shotguns used for deer, turkey, and waterfowl hunting.

Since the gun was featured in magazine photos over the years I'd gone to swathing it in a variety of licensed camouflage tape designs, both to be politically correct with the magazine advertisers and to hide the now-embarrassing green-and-black ornamentation.

Through connections in the industry I was able to get my gun finished by the TarJac company in Waterloo, New York, which did commercial work for Immersion Graphics, a competitor of ColorWorks. The process that TarJac used on new gun and bow parts (and my gun) is today's Second Skin.

The price is comparable to a re-blueing or stock-refinishing job. The pattern also protects the coated pieces from corrosion.

On used guns the parts are thoroughly degreased, then painted with a base coat and primer coat. When both have been dried and taped, a sheet of film is placed on the surface of an immersion tank filled with water heated to a specific temperature. The film, which holds the camouflage pattern, is then sprayed with an activator that dissolves the film, leaving the colors in the water. The part is dipped into the colors, which adhere to the surface.

The Second Skin coating process involves dipping gun parts in a heated bath with a film floating on the surface.

These coated gun parts are headed for the drying area.

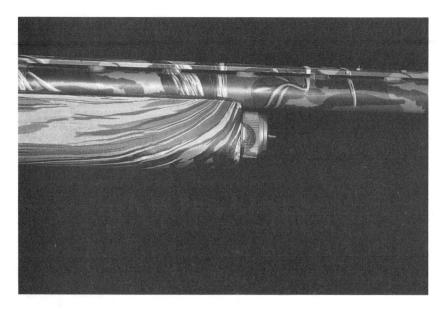

The finished camouflage coating forms a flat, durable, protective shield.

The part is then rinsed, dried, inspected, and sent to a touch-up room.

Second Skin is a subsidiary of Immersion Graphics, a company founded by Realtree camouflage magnate Bill Jordan and a group of investors. The Japanese-designed process was discovered by Steve Lamboy, then Realtree's licensing chief, several years ago at an industry show in Europe.

Second Skin is currently headquartered in Roanoke, Virginia, and is headed by camouflage pioneer Jim Crumley. Interestingly, it is part of an unusual partnership. Crumley started Second Skin when he was still sole owner of Trebark, one of Realtree's main competitors in the commercial camouflage market. Since then, Trebark has been purchased by Mossy Oak's parent company—which today is Realtree's only real competition in the industry. At Second Skin, however, it's just one big happy family.

To find out more about Second Skin, call their headquarters at 540-774-9248 or check out the Web site at www.trebark.com.

THE PERFECT TURKEY GUN

My turkey gun started life as an Ithaca Model 87. The 6½-pound 12-gauge featured a 25-inch, fixed extra-full choke barrel and a mottled paint job that the company felt was ideal camouflage at the time, even though it looked like a third-grade finger-painting project.

I was seeking the perfect turkey gun and this was it—or at least it had potential. Fifteen years, many changes, and more than three dozen gobblers later, it's still a work in progress.

To be honest, right out of the box the gun threw the best turkey pattern (dense core) of any I'd ever encountered. But I'm a tinkerer.

The ultimate turkey gun has several unique features.

If something works well, that doesn't mean that I won't mess with it. So it was with my "Long Tom."

This was before my gunsmithing days, so after a discussion with Joe Morales at Rhino Chokes, I had him lengthen both of the gun's forcing cones, fit a screw-in choke system, and port the barrel. Then I had the barrel cryogenically treated, installed the reworked trigger from my slug gun, and added swivel studs and a sling. A coating of Realtree Xtra-Brown from Second Skin gave it a whole new identity.

Later I added a fiber-optic sighting system and a recoil-reduction device in the stock. Mark Bansner has since made me a choke tube with the right constriction to shoot Remington's Hevi-Shot. I added a Sims Vibration Labs recoil pad and am shopping around for suitable optics to bolt on the receiver for next season.

Magnum Gobble-Dot sight set.

A sling swivel stud drilling jig.

SLINGS

Deer and turkey hunters point their shotguns like rifles and often like to add slings for support and easier carrying. Installing studs for sling swivels is a simple task—made simpler by using a drilling jig, which provides the correct angle with no measuring. The studs screw into the holes and provide steady purchase for the sling swivels.

It's not a good idea to mount studs in the forearms of pumps and semiautos. The alternative is a loop around the barrel at the front end of the sling or a special magazine cap with a stud protruding from it.

Chapter 11

SCOPE MOUNTING

Scopes for shotguns used to hunt deer and turkey are a fairly recent development, but the advent of rifled barrels, high-tech sabot slugs, and exotic turkey loads make them both desirable and necessary. A modern gunsmith needs to know the various facets of mounting a scope on a shotgun and how the process differs from mounting one on a rifle—and he should know how to sight that scope in for the gun's intended use.

You will find that most shotguns don't have the sufficient thickness in the top of the receiver to afford good purchase for mounting screws. Only the Ithaca Model 37, Browning BPS, and precious few others have receivers that can be drilled, tapped, and trusted.

Sporting-goods stores offer a saddle-style, strap-over scope mount that is secured to the receiver with existing screws or pins, but these don't work well. Even the numbest slug shooter will eventually notice that point of impact moves from one shot to the next because it's simply impossible to keep that type of mount perfectly secure.

And if a novice who buys a strap-on mount from a catalog or retail store tries to mount it himself, just removing a receiver pin or screw can lead to a jumble of loose parts inside the receiver

Strap-on scopes are quick and easy to install, but don't provide consistent accuracy.

and a non-functioning firearm that will eventually find its way to the gunsmith.

Instead, mount the scope rail on the receiver by welding or by using a mount that curves over the top of the receiver and mates with the thicker metal where the receiver walls meet the top. One of the best mounts I've seen for semiautomatics and other thin-topped shotgun receivers is produced by Da-Mar Gunsmithing of Solvay, New York.

Always remember to bore-sight any scope you mount in your shop.

SHOTGUN SCOPES ARE DIFFERENT

Because shotguns don't contain their concussion like a thick rifle receiver, they are very tough on scopes. A $39.95 Blue Light Spe-

Mounting a scope on a shotgun is different from attaching a rifle scope.

cial rifle scope can be reduced to a tube of trash by just a couple of slug shots from a shotgun. So all major manufacturers make scopes built especially for shotguns.

However, if you simply must mount a rifle scope (with higher magnification and larger light-gathering objective lens) on a shotgun, it should be a high-quality job that is tested to withstand at least a .375 Magnum pounding. Rifle scopes are commonly adjusted to be parallax-free at 150 yards and shotgun scopes at 50 to 75 yards, but parallax (the displacement of the reticle or crosshairs in relation to the target as the shooter's head moves to either side when aiming) is not a serious concern in slug shooting.

Just as shotguns require special scopes, there are also special considerations for mounting a scope.

THE MOUNTING PROCESS

Let's mount a shotgun scope the right way. Assuming that you have the correct bases and rings (steel, not aluminum) for the scope, the first step is to clean all the screw holes of oil and debris, as well as all the contact surfaces, screws, rings, and bases. I use an aerosol degreaser like Shooter's Choice Quick Scrub III, which doesn't leave a film when it dries.

Many scope mounts use Allen-head hex screws, which afford much better torque (more efficient tightening). They represent a major improvement over slot screws and Phillips heads, but they, too, must be matched with the right-sized wrench. Not just a wrench of the right size, but one with clean, sharp edges that haven't been rounded by overzealous use.

The line between "tight" and "stripped" is a fine one. I have converted virtually all of my base and ring screws to torx heads, a unique six-pointed, star-shaped slot that provides more gripping surface. That means more tightening power without stripping.

Although it's not as much of a problem with shotguns as it is with rifles, you'll sometimes find that the screws that come with bases are not all the same length. Make a dry run, putting the screws in their respective holes and torquing them down to determine if they are too long or too short.

Once you're sure you have the right screws for the right holes, remove them and coat the threads and the contact surfaces of the base and receiver with a locking adhesive like Loctite. Don't just put a drop in the screw hole, as it may keep the screw from bottoming out.

It is imperative to "dedicate" those screws to the receiver, given the mag-

Da-Mar shotgun scope mount.

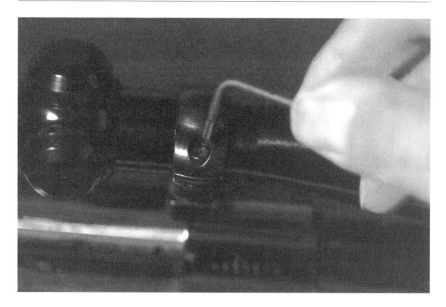

Always use the right tool for the job.

num concussion that they will endure from slug or buckshot loads. Be advised that there are several strengths of Loctite. The super-strength stuff can weld that sucker in place, never to separate. Maybe that's what you want, maybe not. I use lesser-strength Blue Loctite 242 on guns that come to me on loan or that may need a base change at some point.

If the bases are ever to be removed, heating the screw heads with a soldering gun should break the hold. If you are using adjustable rings (from Millett, Weaver, Burris, etc.), the bottom rings should be loosely fastened to the base and aligned using a 1-inch diameter hardwood or aluminum dowel that's 12 inches long. Place the dowel in the rings, check for lateral variation, and adjust as needed.

I like to use a Brownells alignment kit, which consists of two pointed aluminum bars. Install a bar in each ring, with the pointed

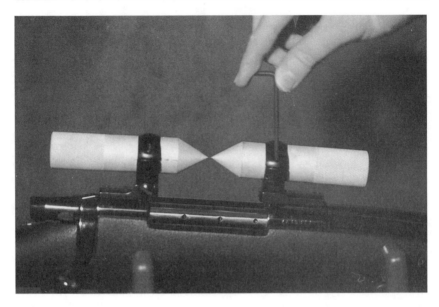

Brownells ring alignment system makes it easier to mount a scope without kinking the tube.

ends facing each other, and align the rings (using alternating screw tension) until the points line up perfectly.

If you are using Leupold, Burris, or Ruger rings that are turned into the base for perfect alignment, use a specialty wrench, aluminum rod, or hardwood dowel in the rings to torque them into place. Never use the scope tube—as obvious as that sounds, I can't tell you the number of times I've seen tubes used as wrenches in this situation.

I am in the process of changing all my bases and rings to the rugged Warne design. Warne rings are solid, square-edged, machined steel that virtually align themselves upon mounting and resist recoil like no other system I've found.

Next—and this is particularly important for scope mounting on heavy-recoiling guns—lap the inside saddles of the rings (top and bottom) with a piece of 320-grit wet-dry sandpaper wrapped around a dowel. I use a lapping bar instead of the dowel to align the rings and administer the lapping process with compound. This assures a larger bearing surface and reduces marring to the scope tube when inserted.

Lap until you've achieved roughly an 80-percent bearing surface on the rings. If you go much more it may actually loosen the tube in the rings. I like to add a dab of rubber cement inside the lapped rings before mounting the scope to further guard against movement.

But before I lay the scope in the rings, I like to center the crosshairs so that I'll have the best possible range of adjustment later. Turn each adjustment dial until it stops, then turn it the other way, counting the clicks until it stops again. Then turn it back half the number of clicks and it's centered.

Lay the scope in the rings, tightening the screws snugly enough to hold it, but not so tight that you can't move the tube in the rings. Tighten screws alternately, first left rear, then right

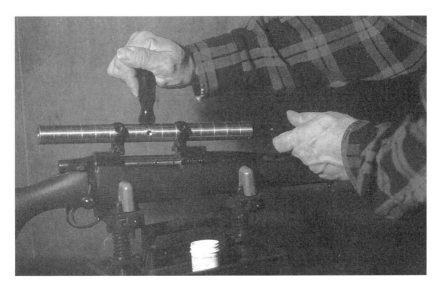

Lap the rings to bear 80 percent on the scope tube.

Stoney Point scope screw substitutes allow you to make ring adjustments without fussing with ring screws or wrenches.

front, then right rear, and so on, turning them the same amount each time to keep the gap between the top and bottom rings equal.

This sytematic screw-tightening rotation not only minimizes the stress on the scope tube but also keeps it square with the barrel. Turning one screw more than another will torque the tube in the rings.

But don't bottom the screws just yet. Leave the scope somewhat loose so that you can adjust for eye relief (at least three inches from scope to brow) and crosshair alignment. Slide the scope forward and back with your head in aiming position (cheek to stock), seeking a bright, complete field of view that is a complete circle. Also adjust the eyepiece so that the crosshairs are totally clear.

You should also align the crosshairs at this point. Everyone looks through a scope with a little different head position, which is why the crosshairs don't look vertical when you look through a friend's scope.

If you're going to adjust your view through the scope, do it with perfectly aligned crosshairs, absolutely vertical and horizontal. For an exact alignment, I like to use a simple gadget called a Reticle Leveler, which saddles over the scope tube and is held in place by rubber bands. Perfect alignment of the crosshairs is essential to long-range accuracy.

Once the eye relief is correct and the crosshairs are aligned, tighten the ring screws, again alternating the tightening until both are torqued down well. You can tell on many adjustable two-piece rings if the pressure is even by comparing the gap in the mating of the top and bottom rings at the side. This is not necessary with Warne, Leupold, Burris, or Ruger rings, which actually cam into alignment when seated.

Next, if you have a collimator (boresighter), align the scope and bore. A variety of laser bore-alignment tools work well in place of a mechanical boresighter, but many need as much as 25 feet of space ahead of the barrel to operate.

If the scope won't "zero" within the limitations of the adjusting turrets, you'll have to pull the whole system apart, place a shim in one of the rings, reassemble, and try again. (I cut up aluminum beverage cans for shims since their wall thickness is about 0.002 inch, which can move the scope's point of aim by an inch at 100 yards.)

ADJUSTING THE SCOPE

It's truly amazing how many slug shooters don't know how, or even if, they should focus their scopes before using them. I'm talking about adjusting the ocular (rear) lens so that the reticle is clear before shooting.

American-style scopes often feature an eyepiece threaded into the scope tube and held in place by a lock ring. To adjust them you must loosen the lock ring and turn the eyepiece in or out until the crosshairs are sharply focused. Be advised that it may take dozens of turns to achieve proper focus. Not so with European designs, which focus by turning the rear rim of the eyepiece, camming the ocular lens in or out. And one turn is usually sufficient.

One tip: Do the focusing at dusk, when your eyes have their shallowest depth of field. You'll focus more precisely.

After the scope has been mounted, focused, and bore-sighted, you should be "on paper" at 25 yards. If you just mounted the scope it may take a couple of shots for it to settle into the rings. Once it's settled, I make preliminary adjustments at 25 yards before fine-tuning at 50 and, under some circumstances, 100 yards.

Remember that when using a scope you should move the reticle in the direction that you want the group to move. For example, if you are grouping left and below the bull's-eye, make the adjustment up and to the right.

Most high-quality rifle scopes adjust at ¼-inch per click at 100 yards. Shotgun scopes, being shorter-range instruments, commonly adjust at ½-inch per click at 100 yards. Check the scope's instructions to determine the adjustment (it's sometimes listed on the turret dial). If it's ¼-inch per click, it takes 8 clicks to move the group 1 inch when shooting at 50 yards; at 25 yards it's 16 clicks.

A common mistake when zeroing a scope is to make adjustments after just one shot. Shoot a group, make the adjustment from the center of the group, and shoot another group to determine if you are zeroed.

Often, especially with cheaper scopes, the adjustment won't register on the next shot; it may take two or three. The reason is that the adjustment spring in some scopes actually rides against the wall of the tube. When you make the adjustment by turning the turret, the spring may or may not wind if it's riding the wall. A shot or two will usually jostle it sufficiently for the adjustment to "take."

This is also one reason you might see someone make an adjustment, then tap the scope tube a few times with a screwdriver or knife handle. But I'm usually leery of hammering scope tubes, even if they don't belong to me.

ADJUSTING OPEN SIGHTS

Moving open sights is different from adjusting scopes. Elevation is usually adjusted with a screw on the side of the sight, or in some cases, by physically moving the sight up or down the mount on steps.

To make windage (lateral) adjustments to iron sights, move the rear sight in the direction that you want the group to move. For example, move the rear sight to the right if you want to move the group to the right.

If you run out of adjustment in the rear sight, windage can still be adjusted by moving the front sight in the direction you want the group to move.

Chapter 12

METAL
TREATMENTS

There are several metal-treating processes involved in gunsmithing that are common yet sufficiently involved in application and equipment that they are usually considered specialty
services. While all gunsmiths should have a general knowledge of
these treatments, few tackle this aspect of gunsmithing themselves.

Only specialists who can afford the overhead, have the
space, and accept the health concerns and hassle of dealing with
local zoning boards, the EPA, and OSHA venture into the three
most common processes that fall under this label—metal blueing, plating, and case hardening.

HOT OR COLD METAL BLUEING

Gun steel is not black. It's actually a shiny silver until the surface
is treated (blued) to make it black. In simple terms, blueing is actually a form of intentional rust that fends off other forms.

Blueing is formed by using a caustic solution to irritate the
surface of the steel so that it forms an oxidized layer. Only steel
can be blued; other metals won't react to the blueing solutions
and require their own specific chemicals for finishing.

The polished metal part placed in a hot-blueing salt bath emerges with a deep, even finish.

The two most common methods used for blueing shotguns are the hot-dip method (utilizing caustic salt solutions) and the rust-blue method. In the hot-dip method the degreased and thoroughly polished parts are immersed in a hot pickling solution of mild acid to remove any surface oxidation, and lead, powder, or plastic remnants. Once clean, the parts are stripped and warmed and immersed in a boiling salt solution.

The temperature of the baths, strength of the solutions, and types of steels involved must be closely monitored. At a certain point the parts are removed from the salts, washed, and soaked in a water-displacing oil bath. The displacement often continues for long periods, which is why a brand-new gun can occasionally be found with white, crusty salt deposits on the surface. That's moisture still being pushed out, and it can simply be brushed off and treated with penetrating oil.

Hot-dip blueing is safe on springs and gun parts, but discolors alloys and case-hardened steels and dissolves solder, aluminum, and brass beads.

The rust-blue method gives a bluer hue to the metal (hot-blue is black) and isn't damaging to solder or brazing. Rust-blueing takes more handwork and tends to be more expensive than hot-dip. Polished parts are degreased and boiled in water, then removed and swabbed with a solution. The blueing occurs in a humidity cabinet. When the parts are removed they are "carded" (scraped) clear of a crusty layer covering the blued steel. The boiling, swabbing, hanging, and carding process is repeated until the blue is sufficiently deep.

After the blued parts are removed from the bath, they are rinsed in a special tank.

The quality of a hot salt solution is directly related to achieving the proper temperature.

Rust-blueing is not cost-effective for small parts and is not done to the bore because the interior can't be effectively carded. The surface is swabbed with Teflon-based lubricant. Brownells developed a process, called Dicropan IM, to get around hot-dip problems and speed up the rust-blue process.

This hot-water process doesn't dissolve solder and brazing like hot-dip, but it does require the disassembly and stripping of parts before immersion, just like the more caustic method.

Due to its expensive and space-consuming nature, blueing is a specialty. And you won't find many old bluers. Business overhead and health concerns tend to do them in.

There is also a cold-blue process that I'd only recommend for touch-ups, although I've used it successfully to blue an entire flintlock shotgun. The finish is not nearly as durable as hot-dip or rust-blue finishes, but the process is much simpler. You simply brush the finish on, let it set for thirty seconds or a minute, and wipe it off. Repeat until it reaches the desired depth or effect.

The metal needs to be polished clean, degreased, then warmed with a light bulb or equivalent heat. The cold-blue solution is swabbed on with a patch, allowed to sit a few minutes, and then rubbed with steel wool. It's then degreased and the process repeated until the blue reaches the desired depth or color. There are also old processes known as nitre and charcoal blueing that require heat transfer and provide a more durable blue than cold-blueing, but these are not as widely used as hot-dip or rust-blueing.

The muzzleloader coating process of "browning" is a rust-blue process that uses different chemicals to produce a brown finish rather than a blue one. Browning is a historic coloring that

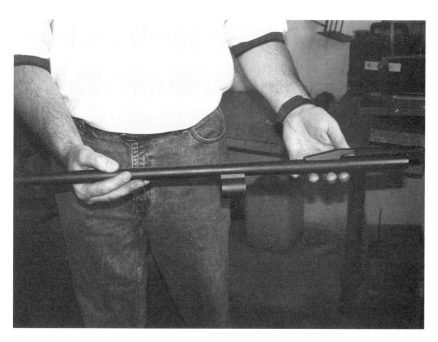

For best results, the hot-blueing process must be followed meticulously.

classic blackpowder gun owners prefer, and the process is done by true specialists. A couple of gunsmiths in my area, Rick Hammond and Jerry Coughlin, were nationally renowned practitioners despite operating small basement shops in their homes.

French Gray finishes are the product of a hot-dip blueing process that is treated with a diluted acid solution to fade the blue to gray.

PLATING PROCESSES

Nickel plating is a very involved and specialized electrochemical deposition process that actually protects better than blueing. But it requires an intermediate base such as copper and lies at an appreciable thickness, which precludes its use on close-fitting parts.

By adding Teflon to the electroless nickel solution, beads of the DuPont miracle product are trapped in a thin layer of e-nickel, improving lubricity.

Another electroless process is Robar's NP3, a silver-gray coating that allows the texture of the metal surface to show through.

"Parkerizing," which is a coating rather than plating, provides a microcrystalline surface that absorbs oil and has the effect of a lubricant reservoir. Parkerizing is achieved by a phosphating solution that takes advantage of a light layer of metal being removed to spark a chemical process that bonds it integrally to the metal.

CASE HARDENING

Case hardening tempers the part, increasing its life (because it doesn't wear as quickly), protecting it from oxidation, and giving it a unique coloration. The process is very involved and potentially deadly, since it involves the use of cyanide, a speck of which in an eye can cause instant death.

The process is intricate and, if applied improperly, can warp the part. It's definitely not a process for hobbyists or small-time gunsmiths. I'm fortunate to have one of the world's best practitioners, Doug Turnbull, operating a few counties away from where I live in New York.

A Turnbull gun is immediately identifiable by the depth and range of its colors and is desired like no other.

SOLDERING, BRAZING, WELDING

There are certain other procedures that gunsmiths need to be knowledgeable about, but may not need to practice, such as soldering, brazing, and welding. Actually, any gunsmith who works on older guns really should learn soldering and brazing, but welding is another story.

All three procedures require absolutely clean surfaces, flux, and the proper amount and type of heat. Thorough cleaning might even mean removal of blueing if, for example, another metal is being sweated to a barrel. The flux prevents oxidation, which occurs when the metal surface is heated—and that heat must be sufficient to make the joining medium flow and to raise the temperature of the parts being joined.

Welding is the strongest joining process for metal, but it requires special equipment, training, and conditions, and is simply not applicable in many gunsmithing situations. Welding requires an acetylene torch or an electric welding outfit, goggles or a mask, a special lighter, gloves, a jacket, and special training. (Welding techniques are not discussed here because the subject is very involved and requires a complete book of its own and hands-on training.)

Silver soldering is necessary when the base metal or something in close proximity can't handle the heat of welding or when logistics don't allow welding. By the same token, it can't be used on aluminum, zinc, or lead because they melt at lower heat than the solder. It is ideal, however, for use on brass, steel, copper, silver, stainless steel, iron, and tungsten carbide.

Silver soldering requires some talent. The secret of all soldering is surface preparation. Scrape it clean, use the right matching flux, and the job is simple. Use the minimum amount of solder—it alloys with the metal surface to provide strength and bonding and excess solder means a weak joint.

Most hardware-store solders are useless for gunsmithing, but there are three types that fulfill most gunsmithing requirements. Silver solder is the strongest and is actually silver brazing—the next best thing to welding in terms of strength. Flat strip and round types, with their matching flux, are the most commonly used.

The flux should be applied to the surfaces being bonded, covering an area about a quarter-inch beyond the joint in all directions. The area is then heated and the solder applied. Silver solder will wick into a joint, regardless of its tightness. The thinner the layer between the two surfaces, the stronger the bond will be. Remarkable stuff.

A heat source is necessary for soldering, and while an oxygen-acetylene torch is handy, a basic propane torch will suffice for gunsmithing applications.

Brownells markets Silvaloy, a soft solder called Force-44 is serviceable for gunsmithing, and their Gunsmiths Solder also lives up to its name.

Chapter 13

_____

THE IMPORTANCE
OF CLEANING

You may be surprised to find that a major facet of gunsmithing lies not in mechanical ability, but in cleaning. Every shotgunner knows that firearms should be cleaned regularly. Of course, we also know the virtues of low-fat foods and flossing too, but how many of us pay attention to them?

Cleaning a shotgun after a day of hunting or shooting is like washing the dishes after a good meal—something that really ought to be done, but which comes at a time when the enjoyment level has waned. Yet the performance of more guns is probably ruined by inattention to cleaning than by all other malfunctions combined.

In fact, the first step in diagnosing or fixing a malfunctioning shotgun should be a thorough cleaning. You'll be amazed how many problems are solved or reduced by a good cleaning.

If you plan to embark on a gunsmithing career, offering a professional cleaning service may attract customers who don't know how, or don't want to be bothered with, thoroughly cleaning a gun, or those who just obtained a used gun with an uncertain history. And those customers may return when they have bigger problems with their shotguns.

WHY CLEAN?

Even after running one hundred trap loads through a gun, I can run a Tico brush, a BoreSnake, or a floor-mounted brush through the barrel and it will look shiny. This will fool most folks into thinking it's clean—but it's not.

The foreign waste elements in your bore—plastic and newly burnished lead—are shiny, too. And they are blending into the barrel shine, hiding there to trap moisture against the steel and compromise the interior surface of the barrel.

Allowing the barrel to stay dirty, or not cleaning ports, also puts a drag on subsequent wads and allows the shot charge to separate before it is supposed to, resulting in blown patterns, high pressures, and excessive recoil. Failing to keep the gas jets clean in an autoloader consistently leads to malfunctions.

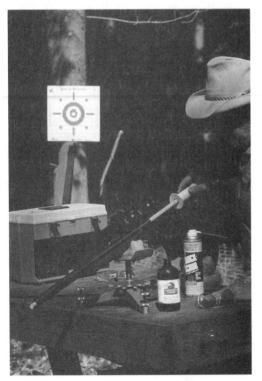

While quite a few of us clean our barrels regularly, only truly experienced shotgunners pay attention to cleaning choke tubes, forcing cones, or chambers, yet that's where pres-

Cleaning a shotgun after a day in the field isn't fun, but it has to be done.

Every gunsmith should have an assortment of cleaning and lubricating agents on hand.

sures are greatest on the shotcup and charge and where plastic fouling builds up the quickest.

Excessive fouling in those areas can really interfere with performance. Clean these areas thoroughly, and you may be credited with being a gunsmithing genius.

I use a Crud Buster tool to clean choke tubes and a chamber brush to scour that potential problem area. One tip: Once you install the chamber brush on the handle, don't take it off. It has a larger diameter than a conventional barrel brush, but looks the same and can be compressed (and thus ruined) by inadvertent use in the bore.

Be advised that rifled-barrel shotguns that fire sabot slugs will likely have fairly clean bores. The slug never touches the barrel interior and the only barrel fouling will be powder residue ahead of the chamber. If the barrel is ported, however, plastic will build up as it gets shaved off passing sabots by the edges of the ports, and that buildup can affect accuracy.

BORES

Let's start with the bore. Riflemen are usually warned to stay away from hardened or stainless-steel jointed rods because they can scratch a bore and mar rifling. Since shotgun barrel steel is even softer than rifle steel, it makes sense to avoid these rods, as well.

Jointed aluminum rods are similarly unhealthy because a soft metal like aluminum can pick up grit and act just like a lap, scratching the lands and grooves of a rifled barrel or the mirror finish of a shotgun tube with every stroke. I use only nylon-coated rods from Dewey or Bore Tech.

For 12-gauge shotguns, an excellent patch rod can be made from a ⅝-inch wooden dowel with a bicycle handlebar grip fastened to one end. An absorbent paper towel (Bounty brand seems to work best) folded and rolled to bore-filling diameter is an excellent shotgun cleaning patch.

Soak the towel with bore solvent and push it the length of the bore from chamber to muzzle. Then work a bronze brush, tornado brush, or even a bore brush wrapped with a copper kitchen scrubbie that's been wetted with bore solvent through the bore, paying special attention to the choke and forcing cone.

Next, run a wet patch through, and follow it with dry patches until they emerge clean. If you are looking to remove plastic wad or sabot fouling use a little common sense and avoid solvents that come in a plastic bottle. If it doesn't eat through

Bore swabs and quality bronze brushes are essential for cleaning shotgun barrels.

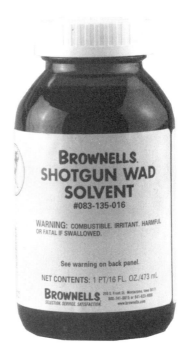

Brownells shotgun wad solvent.

Quality bore solvent is expensive, but it's a good investment because it can be used repeatedly.

a plastic container, it won't melt away wad fouling.

Also, use only phosphorus bronze brushes wound on a core for shotguns. Stainless-steel brushes are so hard they will score the steel in some shotgun barrels.

Stubborn fouling may require a vigorous scrubbing with a brush or scrubbie. In badly fouled bores I use a motorized power scrubber from Outers. Before I found this, I used to score a rod and wrap it with steel wool, then put the rod in a drill chuck to use as a rotary scrubber.

Badly fouled gas ports in autoloaders can be very frustrating to clean. I like to soak them in bore solvent a couple of days before tackling the job with a gas-ring or barrel-hanger brush. I've seen gas systems so encrusted that it took a grinding tool to dislodge the crud.

If I'm going to be storing the gun for a while I might run a wet patch through the cleaned barrel to leave a protective film— just remember to swab it out before shooting again.

I keep a stainless-steel barrel tank filled with solvent year-round and soak my trap (and occasionally my slug gun) barrels in it before giving them a thorough cleaning. Any surface rust can be rubbed off with fine steel wool. I realize that buying a couple of gallons of bore solvent is a pretty serious investment, but the stuff lasts for years.

A trapshooting friend of mine makes an affordable and serviceable (yet caustic) alternative known as Ed's Red Bore Cleaner. (See the sidebar below for more on Ed's Red.) Surface rust can be lifted cleanly from barrels and receivers soaked in this stuff with just a fine steel-wool pad.

You won't want to use this concoction in a confined shop, but it works wonders in well-ventilated areas. My friend once filled a parts washer with the mixture and left some parts in it overnight. The next day he turned on the washer motor and got no response. The concoction had dissolved the motor's plastic housing and the resultant gunk buggered the motor.

Remember that the cleaning rods should always be wiped clean and the brushes should have solvent rinsed out of them with a degreasing agent. Solvent is meant to dissolve gilded metal and doesn't know the difference between residue and bronze or brass bristles.

THE CLEANING CRADLE

Always use a cleaning cradle to hold the firearm or barrel steady while you work the cleaning rod. The cradle should have padding to protect the finish and should be built so that the muzzle is lower than the breech, which allows solvents to drain away from the chamber and the wooden stock.

MTM Caseguard makes a quality, low-lying "portable maintenance station" that I've used for years. It's designed to sit piggyback on a portable tool chest. Tipton also makes a version designed for field use that is an actual tool chest that opens into a cradle.

CHOKE TUBES

Screw-in choke tubes also require special attention. If they are ported, they will definitely need to be scrubbed regularly with a specialty tool like a Crud Buster and a choke tube cleaner like Shooter's Choice to get rid of wad or sabot fouling scraped off by the ports. Even non-ported tubes need extra scrubbing because they catch the full brunt of a slug being slammed through at peak velocity, which is bound to shave and shape that slug.

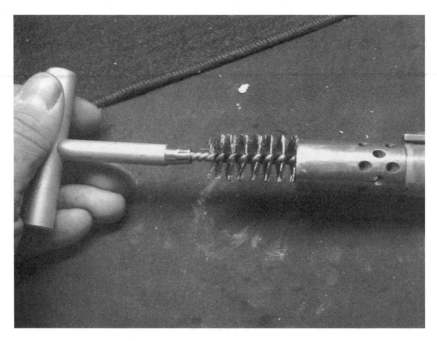

A Crud Buster choke tube brush.

ED'S RED, HOMEMADE BORE CLEANER

Competitive shooters have a history of concocting alternatives to high-priced commercial solvents. And one of the most effective homemade bore solvent/cleaning agents I've ever encountered is Ed's Red, a solvent recipe adapted by well-known shooting industry figure Ed Harris, who worked with Ruger and the military.

A shooting buddy showed me a piece that Harris wrote on Ed's Red Bore Cleaner in the mid-1990s, and I now keep a bath of it in a covered stainless-steel barrel soaking tray in an outbuilding year-round. This stuff is caustic and flammable and should only be used outside or in a well-ventilated area—a description that basically defines my breezy backyard workshop.

Proper precautions should be taken and directions should be followed exactly, but when mixed and used correctly, this stuff is quite effective at dissolving carbon residue, cleansing the barrel, and protecting the steel finish against corrosion. And it costs a fraction of the price of commercial bore solvents.

Harris's recipe, which is now in the public domain, is based on proven principles and incorporates two polar and two non-polar ingredients. It is adapted from a formula in Hatcher's Notebook, Frankford Arsenal Cleaner No. 18, but substituting equivalent modern materials.

Harris had the presence of mind to solicit the input of an organic chemist so that there would be no "surprises" in the end product.

MIXING INSTRUCTIONS

The ingredients in Ed's Red are as follows: one part Dexron II, IIe, or III ATF (GM Spec. D-20265 or later); one part deodorized, K1 kerosene; one part Aliphatic Mineral Spirits (Fed. Spec. TT-T-2981F, CAS #64741-49-9, or substitute Stoddard Solvent, CAS #8052-41-3, or Varsol); and one part acetone (CAS #67-64-1).

An optional ingredient is one pound of lanolin, anhydrous, USP per gallon. (It's OK to substitute Lanolin, the modified, topical lubricant available at drug stores.) Ed's Red works well without the lanolin, but incorporating it makes the cleaner easier on the hands and provides better residual lubrication and corrosion protection if you plan to use it for long-term storage. If you want to minimize cost, you can skip the lanolin and save about eight bucks per gallon.

Mix the ingredients outdoors or in an area with good ventilation. Use a clean, one-gallon, metal, chemical-resistant, heavy-gauge PET or PVC plastic container. NFPA-approved plastic gasoline storage containers are also fine. Do *not* use HDPE, which is breathable, because the acetone will evaporate. The acetone will also attack HDPE in about six months, making a heck of a mess.

Add the Dexron ATF first. Use the empty container to measure the other components, so that it gets thoroughly rinsed. If you incorporate lanolin into the mixture, melt this carefully in a double boiler, taking precautions against fire. Pour the melted lanolin into a larger container, rinsing the container with the bore-cleaner mix and stirring until it is all dissolved.

Harris recommended diverting a small quantity, up to four ounces per quart, of the 50-50 ATF/kerosene mix for use as an "ER-compatible" gun oil. This can be done without impairing the effectiveness of the final mix.

If you are using Ed's Red as a solvent on a patch, leaving it to soak for at least a minute after application will improve its function. Harris said that leaving the bore wet will protect it from rust for up to thirty days, and that if the lanolin is incorporated into the mixture it will protect the firearm from rust for up to two years.

You should wipe spilled Ed's Red from exterior surfaces before storing the gun. While Ed's Red is said to be harmless to blued and nickel finishes, the acetone will eat at most wood finishes.

ACTIONS

While many shotgunners put their firearms away when the barrel is clean, that's only part of a thorough cleaning. You should be familiar enough with any shotgun you use regularly to take it apart and clean the action, trigger mechanism, and interior surfaces.

This requires a long screwdriver or socket wrench and extension (to pull the stock), screwdrivers and drift or pin punches to disassemble the receiver, and maybe a spanner wrench if you're pulling the forearm off a pump.

Old lubricant and carbon and primer fouling are magnets for airborne crud, which accumulates inside the receiver faster than outside. After disassembling the gun, use a toothbrush to scrub bearing surfaces with bore solvent.

Sometimes a misbehaving shotgun just needs a thorough cleaning.

I've recently begun spraying the works with an aerosol action cleaner, letting it drain off into a wad of paper towels, and wiping it off and spraying with a degreaser. I then coat the metal surfaces with a quality moisture displacent.

Because bore solvent is so expensive, some folks use mineral spirits to wash parts and scrub actions. Mineral spirits are inexpensive, non-flammable, not petroleum based, and virtually odorless when new. After this cleaning solution has been used for a while, an odor develops from the traces of kerosene in its makeup, but the liquid is easy to dispose of.

I like to wash parts in Brownells d'Solve, a concentrate that can be mixed with water to create a very effective, yet non-caustic, cleaning solvent. I know that water is the Devil's own tool when it comes to firearms, but parts washed and scrubbed in a water-based solvent can be dried with a hair dryer or heat gun. They should then be wiped with penetrating oil. These two steps are unnecessary if your cleaning solvent is petroleum-based, however.

LUBRICATION IS OVERRATED

In many cleaning situations, lubrication is overrated, and may well be more detrimental than helpful. When breaking in a new gun, a small amount of lubricant may ease the wear on metal-to-metal contact areas, but most shotgunners use too much. Excess lubricant can gum up the action by attracting grime or actually impede the action when it changes consistency in extreme temperatures.

If a particular brand of grease is rated for extreme temperatures, its label will likely proclaim the fact prominently. If not, beware. Chances are, you're holding something that turns into gunk in extremely cold weather. I use Shooter's Choice high-temperature grease, which is tested to retain its viscosity in temperatures that range from oven-hot to severely cold.

When using a grease or oil lubricant the rule of thumb is, "If you can see it, it's too much." Use lubricant sparingly, and always check the temperature range on the product label.

STORING GUNS

A gun exposed to extreme elements—whether going from a cold duck blind or treestand to a warm cabin or from bright sunshine into an air-conditioned vehicle—will likely be wet. And water is an obvious enemy when it's allowed to sit on metal.

In these situations, all guns should be wiped down thoroughly with a dry cloth, disassembled to get at ambient moisture in the interior, and then sprayed liberally with a moisture-displacing agent such as Shooter's Choice Rust Prevent. Apply one coat, let it sit for thirty seconds, and then wipe it off. Spray a second, lighter coat before putting the gun away in its case or vault.

As mentioned earlier, I like to run a solvent-soaked patch or a patch soaked with Rust Prevent down a clean barrel before storing the gun. Again, be sure to swab any residue from the barrel before using it again.

I keep fresh silica bags in my gun vaults at all times to discourage rusting, and I keep a vigilant eye on the moisture-monitoring strips to know when to replace the bags.

Chapter 14

CUSTOM
HANDLOADING

S ome professional gunsmithing shops now offer handloading for specialty shotshells, and it's something even amateur gunsmiths can do to maximize the performance of a particular gun. Loading custom nontoxic waterfowl loads, slugs, buckshot, and even target loads for a specific gun can be rewarding, and it doesn't require a major investment in equipment or special training. For instance, if you have a shotgun with a bore that differs significantly (tighter or looser) from conventional bores of the same gauge, it will pattern differently. A specific handload can be created to fit that particular bore so it patterns the way the shooter wants.

Excellent commercial ammunition is widely available today, but there's always someone looking for something a little different. You can't, for instance, find 28-gauge slugs or 10-gauge sabots or hard-hitting .410 loads in stores, but you can handload them.

Many hunters and competition shooters balk at the prices of commercial ammo or want personal loads tailored for specific uses. Competitive trap-, skeet, and sporting-clays shooters often use expensive, high-performance Federal Gold Medal, Winchester AA, or Remington STS Premier loads—but the same thing, in

A modern progressive reloader like the RCBS Grand can produce a full case or more of custom-loaded shotgun shells in an hour.

the same hulls, can be loaded for a substantially lower price. All it takes is a modest investment and a little research and elbow grease.

Catalog houses like Ballistic Products, Inc. (BPI) and Precision Reloading offer specialty components, instructions, books, load data, and equipment to bring everything from cheap practice loads to the most obscure specialty loads within reach of handloaders.

Your biggest cash outlay will be the purchase of reloading equipment, a decent progressive press, some extra powder, and shot bushings, but this cost can be amortized over years of loading or paid off in short order if you build a decent business.

My RCBS Grand progressive press cost less than five hundred dollars and is the cleanest operating, most efficient shotshell press I've ever seen. It can easily load a case of shotshells in an hour—300 or 350 if I'm in a good rhythm—and I'm counting on a lifetime of use.

NOT FOR EVERYONE

Of course, reloading is not for everyone. If you must smoke, have distractions nearby, are naturally careless or daring, or if you're the type who doesn't read directions until after you get into trouble, you are much better off staying away from reloading.

A mature, sensible approach is essential. If you understand the fact that components are not interchangeable and that the reloading process must be conducted with extreme care, thought, and precision, you are a candidate for reloading.

Unlike metallic cartridge reloading, each shotshell load carries with it specific and absolute components that must be used. If you can get a good buy on Brand A wads as opposed to the specified Brand B, you can't use them unless you find a load specifying Brand A.

Don't listen to what your well-intentioned but under-informed salesclerk or buddy says about interchangeability of components. If you are bargain hunting, take along a reloading manual to determine if data exists for the components you want to buy.

It's best to use unibody (one-piece) hulls like Winchester AA, Federal Gold Medal, or Remington STS because of their quality and simplicity and because you won't have to add a basewad.

THE LOADING PROCESS

The actual process of loading shotshells, including buckshot, is pretty straightforward. Let's look at a non-progressive press first, the simplest available. This type of press loads one shell at a time, the shell manually moved from die station to die station until all the operations have been performed.

The case body and metal head is full-length resized; the fired primer removed (decapping); a new primer seated (priming); the powder charge dropped; the wad seated; shot charge dropped (slugs have to be hand-inserted); the crimp started; and the final crimp applied.

You may want to use a specialized roll-crimper for slugs. While there may be minor operational differences among presses, these are likely minor and will be covered in the instructional manual that comes with each press.

Progressive presses perform all the same functions, in the same relative order, as non-progressive presses, but the functions are performed on each pull of the lever at different stations on different hulls.

The loading process in a progressive press starts with the tool shell plate empty. You insert a case, perform the first step, advance the shell plate, insert a second case, perform two operations, and so on until the press has six cases in the shell plate—one positioned at each station. You just need to keep feeding

It's not difficult to create custom handloads, but it does require strong attention to detail.

cases and components in order to obtain a fully loaded round for each down-up stroke of the press handle.

Loading begins at the left front of the tool, progresses counterclockwise, and the finished round is removed from the nine o'clock position.

Even modest efforts on most non-progressive presses will yield the reloader one hundred or more shotshell rounds per hour, although it's much slower with slugs. Progressive presses can load around three times that number per hour.

HANDLOADING SLUGS

Handloading slugs with a rolled crimp—the most efficient method for solid performance but the biggest pain in terms of actual loading—is essentially a one-at-a-time proposition. The roll crimp is preferable for slug loads because of the uneven crimping surface provided by the nose of the slug.

For roll-crimping, the hull must be secured in a Hull Vise and wad pressure set at 40 pounds to ensure proper wad seating, and the evacuation of air between the powder and the wad.

In most cases the wads are partially sealed into the hull, then the slug inserted into the sabot, followed by the 40-pounds seating process, and completed by crimping.

Roll-crimping requires a smooth hull mouth and, as just noted, you aren't going to get that with a folded crimp hull. The Hull Vise and hull should be positioned on a drill-press table and the roll-crimp starter (inserted in the drill chuck) slowly lowered into the mouth of the hull. The friction generated from the spinning tool will soften the crimp. Too slow or too fast and you'll likely screw up the process. Experts note that 300 rpm is ideal, but how do you measure that? With a little practice, however, you'll discern the right speed and the correct amount of down pressure.

You can use 3-inch, fold-crimped hulls as 2¾-inch slug hulls for roll-crimping by trimming ¼-inch at the bottom of the fold crimp. It's still much better, though, to use roll-crimped production slug hulls to make roll-crimped handloads.

Slug hulls are shorter than the shotshell variety because the shorter crimp makes it easier to get the slug out of the hull efficiently. You'll also find that you'll never get good performance from other star-crimped hulls cut for roll-crimping.

Good hulls can easily be reloaded five or six times, sometimes as many as ten times if the loads are not too severe. In fact, the performance of handloads that used commercial slug hulls can even get demonstrably better after two or three loadings of a particular hull, sometimes dropping the standard deviation to less than 5 feet per second. The plastic in the hulls is losing resiliency and conforming to the specific dimensions of that shotgun chamber.

In effect, they are fire-formed like rifle brass, which expands to precisely fit a particular gun's chamber. But I suspect that another factor of the repeated firings plays a larger role than chamber fit. The slug's crimp is critical to performance, and after a couple of loadings and firings the crimp fold will lose its stiffness and open with less resistance upon ignition. Sort of like breaking in a new pair or shoes.

There is obviously a limit to the life of a reloaded hull, though, and you should inspect each one closely after every firing. Check for interior damage from the powder burn and exterior flaws made by an ejector arm or maybe from being crushed underfoot. Also, check the basewad. It should be tight and not missing any chunks. Shape-up tools are great for inserting and working around the crimp area, relaxing the folds and giving the loader more room to work with.

FOLLOW THE RECIPE EXACTLY

Even with slugs, every load takes a specific primer. Substituting one primer for another can diminish or exaggerate performance and almost certainly will alter interior ballistics, which ain't good.

Powders are tailored to load objectives. Slug weight, velocity goals, and expected air temperatures are all factors when selecting a powder. Cold-temperature slugs and lighter slugs require faster burning powders for consistent burns. Use a slow-burning powder to tweak a light slug to high velocity only when conditions are acceptable.

Sealing wads differ with various combinations of slug and powder. In many cases, conventional cushioned shotcup wads can be used as sabots for rifled-barrel loads. Whatever wad you use must seal the gases behind the slug to provide consistency.

The safe handloader follows proven recipes exactly.

If you're using a fold crimp, it must be pushed open from the exact center or the slug will be tilted when it enters the barrel. Depending on the style of the slug, it may be difficult to align the nose perfectly every time, which is why overshot wads are necessary. It brings the point of force off the outside edge rather than the slug nose.

Some loads, particularly those designed for smoothbores, require Teflon wrappers around the slug to make the projectile conform more tightly to the barrel. They seem to improve accuracy and reduce deformation of the slug.

Always consider what the air temperature will be when you are actually shooting the slugs. Powder loses energy when the air gets colder. There's no fixed variable for this, though; each powder type and burn rate is different.

If you are loading at 70 degrees Fahrenheit but are looking for performance at 30 degrees, you'll obviously need to make the load slightly hotter. Fast-burning powders lose less energy with falling temperatures, slow-burning powders lose more, probably because the pressure curve is spread out more and the energy delivered over a longer period of time. If that pressure is not maintained, due to energy loss during cold temperatures, the burning cycle is hampered and consistency and energy are lost.

Low chamber pressure and a large amount of free bore make consistent slug accuracy problematical. When you think about it, you have to wonder why today's slugs shoot as well as they do.

Consider the chamber fit. A 2¾-inch slug actually unfolds to about 2⅝ inches. In a 3-inch chamber, which is what you find in 99 percent of all commercial slug guns, that means a ⅜-inch jump from the 0.809-inch-diameter chamber to the throat of the 0.729-diameter (0.718 in a rifled-bore) barrel. If you have a 3½-inch chamber, that's ⅞ inch of free bore! Imagine that scenario in a rifle.

This is the case with Foster-style or short slugs. Actually, the rear of sabot and attached-wad slugs is still in the hull or very shortly removed, which means it's evenly supported when the nose of the slug reaches the throat of a 3-inch chamber. But in a 3½-inch chamber it's pretty much a leap of faith.

In fact, Lightfield recommends against shooting its 2¾-inch Hybred sabots in 3½-inch chambers (only the Mossberg 835 and Remington 11–87 offer rifled bores with that size chamber) for fear that the thin-walled sabot halves will be dislodged from the slug while it traverses the free bore and will be jammed back together when the projectile hits the throat.

Although the scenario has never created any catastrophes, it certainly can cause a pressure spike and—at the very least—a healthy jolt of recoil.

WHAT'S AVAILABLE NOW

Ballistic Products, Inc. (BPI) of Minnesota is the premier source for slug and buckshot handloading components, supplies, manuals, molds, powder, primers, loading tools, and virtually anything else the handloader could need or want. And they have plenty of stuff you won't find anywhere else.

Precision Reloading of Connecticut is also a leading shotshell component company and recently entered into the shotgun slug business, marketing the Lyman and Sabot Technologies' HammerHead slugs, among others.

Today, there are still dozens of slug designs available to handloaders that are sufficiently weird to keep major manufacturers from loading them, yet still fill myriad shooting niches. Lightfield Hybreds, Barnes Expander SGS, Gualandi and Chris Young's Collett Cup slugs—all of which are also loaded commercially—are available as projectiles through BPI. The Italian-made Gualandi attached-wad slug, which is loaded commercially by a couple of companies, is available in several sizes through BPI, as is the similarly designed 0.735-inch-diameter, 1 ⅛-ounce Thunderbolt. BPI sells the one-ounce, 0.735-inch-diameter 12-gauge Mexican-made Aquila (AQ) slugs too, which feature nylon gear-like fins that are supposed to impart a stabilizing rotation.

You can also find cast round balls in diameters of 0.690 (487 grains) and 0.715 (550 grains) that fit inside conventional shotcups like sabots.

BPI markets a frangible Foster-style slug called the Defender in 10-gauge (0.660 diameter, 1.5 ounce) and 20-gauge (0.615 diameter, ⅞ ounce), and something called an Improved Foster, which is essentially a big wadcutter design with a polished nose that supposedly reduces drag. It's available in 10-, 12-, and 28-gauge.

Another small-gauge specialty load is the Light Game Slug, an attached-wad design that comes in 28-gauge (0.505 diameter, 183 grains) and .410 (0.375 diameter, 93 grains). Lyman offers an hourglass-shaped slug for handloaders and also sells molds for it. Lee makes a slug mold, too.

Precision Reloading offers specific recipes for the Sabot Technologies' HammerHead, a one-ounce, non-discarding sabot slug similar to the Lightfield Commander design. The heavy sabot is a major advantage in that it gives the load a very high ballistic coefficient and can be loaded with a variety of slugs (lead, tungsten, copper, etc.) that make it appealing for special-use applications such as piercing armor, doors, or windshields.

STORING AMMUNITION

Despite what you've seen in the movies, firearm ammunition stocks will not mass explode. According to the Sporting Arms and Ammunition Manufacturers Institute (SAAMI), if a single cartridge or shotshell in a carton or case is caused to fire, it will not cause other adjacent cartridges or shotshells to explode simultaneously.

Firearm ammunition is simply not an overly sensitive item. It won't explode due to shock or excessive vibration, and if somehow discharged in the open without the support provided by a firearm's chamber or other close confinement, it explodes very inefficiently.

If a cartridge explodes outside the chamber, the projectile or debris particles from the case or hull have an extremely limited velocity and range. The only types of debris likely to be flung far are pieces of the primer cap, which may be propelled a short range, usually under 50 feet.

APPENDIX: SHOTGUN AND GUNSMITHING RESOURCES

GUNSMITHING SUPPLIES

Brownells, Inc.
200 South Front Street
Montezuma, IA 50171
1-800-741-0015; 641-623-5401
www.brownells.com

MidwayUSA
5875 West Van Horn
  Tavern Road
Columbia, MO 65203
1-800-243-3220; 573-445-6363
www.midwayusa.com

Numrich Arms
Gun Parts Division
226 Williams Lane
West Hurley, NY 12491
1-866-686-7424; 845-679-2417
www.e-gunparts.com

SHOTGUN MAKERS

Benelli-Stoeger-Franchi
17603 Indian Head Hwy.
Accokeek, MD 20607
301-283-6981
www.benelliusa.com
www.franchiusa.com

Beretta USA
17601 Beretta Drive
Accokeek, MD 20607
301-283-2191
www.berettausa.com

Browning
One Browning Place
Morgan, UT 84050
801-876-2711
www.browning.com

Charles Daly
K.B.I. Inc.
P.O. Box 6625
Harrisburg, PA 17112
1-866-DALYGUN
www.charlesdaly.com

European American Armory
P.O. Box 1299
Sharpes, FL 32959
321-639-4842
www.eaacorp.com

Heckler & Koch, Inc.
(Fabarms)
21480 Pacific Blvd.
Sterling, VA 22170–8903
703-450-1900
www.hecklerkoch-usa.com

Ithaca Gun
901 Route 34B
King Ferry, NY 13081
1-888-9-ITHACA
www.ithacagun.com

Marlin Firearms Co.
100 Kenna Drive
North Haven, CT 06473
203-239-5621
www.marlinfirearms.com

New England Firearms
Co., Inc.
(also H&R 1871)
Industrial Rowe
Gardner, MA 01440
978-632-9393

O. F. Mossberg & Sons, Inc.
7 Grasso Avenue
North Haven, CT 06473
203-230-5300
www.mossberg.com

Remington Arms Co., Inc.
870 Remington Drive
P.O. Box 700
Madison, NC 27025-0700
1-800-243-9700
www.remington.com

Savage Arms, Inc.
118 Mountain Road
Suffield, CT 06078
1-800-235-1821
www.savagearms.com

SKB Shotguns
4325 South 120th Street
Omaha, NE 68137
1-800-752-2767
www.skbshotguns.com

Tar-Hunt Slug Guns
101 Dogtown Road
Bloomsburg, PA 17815
570-784-6368
www.tar-hunt.com

Traditions Performance
 Firearms
1375 Boston Post Road
Old Saybrook, CT 06475

1-860-388-4656
www.traditionsfirearms.com

U.S. Repeating Arms
(Winchester Firearms)
275 Winchester Avenue
Morgan, UT 84050–9333
801-876-3440
www.winchester-guns.com

Weatherby, Inc.
3100 El Camino Real
Atascadero, CA 93422
1-800-227-2016
www.weatherby.com

CHOKE TUBES AND BARRELS

Anderson Custom
170 Antioch Road
Batesville, AR 72501
1-866-307-0500
keith@customshotguns.com

Stan Baker Barrels
10000 Lake City Way
Seattle, WA 98125
206-522-4575

Angle Porting
By Ballistic Specialties
P.O. Box 2401
Batesville, AR 72503
1-800-276-2550
www.angleport.com

Bansner's Custom Gunsmithing
261 East Main Street
Adamstown, PA19501
717-484-2370

Briley Manufacturing
1230 Lumpkin
Houston, TX 77043
1-800-331-5718
www.briley.com

Carlson's
P.O. Box 162
Atwood, KS 67730
785-626-3700

Cation
(Sniper choke tubes)
2341 Alger Street
Troy, MI 48083
810-689-0658
cation@mich.com

Clear View Products
3021 N. Portland
Oklahoma City, OK 73107
405-943-9222

Colonial Arms
1109C Singleton Dr.
Selma, AL 36702
1-800-949-8088
www.colonialarms.com

Comp-N-Choke
925 Waynesboro Highway
Sylvania, GA 30467

1-888-875-7906
www.comp-n-choke.com

Hastings Barrels
320 Court Street
P.O. Box 224
Clay Center, KS 67432
785-632-2184
www.hastingsbarrels.com

Haydel's Game Calls
5018 Hazel Jones Road
Bossier City, LA 71111
1-800-HAYDELS
www.haydels.com

Ithaca Gun Barrels
901 Route 34B
King Ferry, NY 13081
1-888-9-ITHACA
www.ithacagun.com

Kick's Industries
925 Waynesboro Highway
Sylvania, GA 30467
1-888-587-2779
www.kicks-ind.com

Marble Arms/Poly-Choke
P.O. Box 111
Gladstone, MI 49837
906-428-3710

Nu-Line Guns
1053 Caulks Hill Road
Harvester, MO 63304
636-441-4500
nulineguns@nulineguns.com

Patternmaster
6431 North Taos Road
Scott City, KS 67871
620-872-3022

Rhino Chokes
21890 NE Highway 27
Williston, FL 32696
1-800-226-3613
rhinoman@atlantic.net

Seminole Gunworks
3049 U.S. Route 1
Mims, FL 32754
1-800-980-3344
www.seminolegun.com

Tru-Glo
13745 Neutron Drive
Dallas, TX 75244
972-774-0300
www.truglosights.com

Trulock Chokes
102 E. Broad Street

Whigham, GA 31797
1-800-293-9402
www.trulockchokes.com

Walker's Game Ear
P.O. Box 1069
Media, PA 19063
610-565-8952
www.walkersgameear.com

Wright's, Inc.
4591 Shotgun Alley
Pinckneyville, IL 62274
618-357-8933
www.wrightschokes.com

National Rifle Association
11250 Waples Mill Road
Fairfax, VA 22030
703-267-1000
www.nra.org

Sporting Arms & Ammunition
  Manufacturers Institute
  (SAAMI)
11 Mile Hill Road
Flintlock Ridge Office
  Center
Newton, CT 06470
203-426-1320
www.saami.org

GUN CARE PRODUCTS

300-Below Cryogenic
 Tempering
2999 Parkway Drive
Decatur, IL 62526
217-423-3070
www.300below.com

Birchwood Casey
7900 Fuller Road
Eden Prairie, MN 55344
1-800-328-6156
www.birchwoodcasey.com

Bore Tech, Inc.
2950 N. Advance Lane
Colmar, PA 18915
215-997-9689
www.boretech.com

BoreSnake
GunMate
P.O. Box 1720
Oregon City, OR 97045
503-655-2837

Break-Free Inc.
An Armor Holdings Company
13386 International Pkwy.
Jacksonville, FL 32218

1-800-428-0588
www.break-free.com

Chem-Pak, Inc.
242 Corning Way
Martinsburg, WV 25401
1-800-336-9828
www.chem-pak.com

Choke Shine
G.E.M.S., Inc.
33717 Highway 23
Collins, GA 30421
1-888-507-8762
www.chokeshine.com

Corrosion Technologies
P.O. Box 551625
Dallas, TX 75355–1625
1-800-638-7361
corrosnx@ix.netcom.com

J. Dewey Rods
P.O. Box 2104
Southbury, CT 06488
203-264-3064

DSX Products
M.S.R., Inc.

P.O. Box 1372
Sterling, VA 20167–1372
1-800-822-0258

Du-Lite Corp.
171 River Road
Middletown, CT 06457
860-347-2505

EEZOX Inc.
P.O. Box 772
Waterford, CT 06385
1-800-462-3331

Flitz International
821 Mohr Avenue
Waterford, WI 53185
1-800-558-8611
www.flitz.com

Free Gun Cleaner
Frigon Guns
1605 Broughton Road
Clay Center, KS 67432
785-632-5607

Golden Bore Gun Care
Termark International
200 W. 17th Street
Cheyenne, WY 82001
1-888-483-7677
goldenbore@usa.net

H&R Outdoors
914 Artic Street
Bridgeport, CT 06608
1-888-761-4250

Hoppes
Div. of Michaels of Oregon
Airport Industrial Mall
Coatesville, PA 19320
610-384-6000
www.hoppes.com

The Inhibitor
Van Patten Industries
P.O. Box 6694
Rockford, IL 61125
815-332-4812
www.theinhibitor.com

International Lubrication
  Labs
1895 East 56 Road
Lecompton, KS 66050
785-887-6004

Iosso Products
1485 Lively Blvd.
Elk Grove, IL 60007
847-437-8400
www.iosso.com

Kleen-Bore, Inc.
16 Industrial Pkwy.
Easthampton, MA 01027
1-800-445-0301

Mpro7 Gun Care
Windfall, Inc.
P.O. Box 54988
225 W. Deer Valley Rd. #4
Phoenix, AZ 85078
1-800-YES-4MP7

Ms. Moly Ballistic
  Conditioner
1952 Knob Road
Burlington, WI 53105
1-800-264-4140

MTM Molded Products
3370 Obco Court
Dayton, OH 45413
513-890-7461

Neco
536 C. Stone Road
Benicia, CA 94510
707-747-0897

Otis Technology
P.O. Box 582
Lyons Falls, NY 13368

1-800-OTISGUN
www.otisgun.com

Outers
P.O. Box 38
Onalaska, WI 54650
608-781-5800

Ox-Yoke Originals
34 West Main Street
Milo, ME 04463
207-943-7351

Peak Enterprises
79 Bailey Drive
Newman, GA 30263
770-253-1397
tpeak@west.ga.net

Pro-Shot Products
P.O. Box 763
Taylorsville, IL 62568
217-824-9133
www.proshotproducts.com

Prolix
Div. of ProChemCo
P.O. Box 1348
Victorville, CA 92393–1348
760-243-3129
prolix@accex.net

ProTec International
1747 Bartlett Road
Memphis, TN 38134
1-800-843-5649, ext. 101
sales@proteclubricants.com

Rapid Rod
ATSKO, Inc.
2664 Russell Street
Orangeburg, SC 29115
1-800-845-2728
info@atsko.com

Rig Products
56 Coney Island Drive
Sparks, NV 89509
775-359-4451

Rusteprufe Labs
1319 Jefferson Avenue
Sparta, WI 54656
608-269-4144
rusteprufe@centurytel.net

Salvo Industries
5173 N. Douglas Fir Road
Calabasas, CA 91302
818-222-2276
jacob@ammotech.com

Sentry Solutions
111 Sugar Hill Road
Contoocook, NH 03229
603-746-5687
bwc@sentrysolutions.com

Shooter's Choice Gun Care
Ventco Industries
15050 Berkshire Industrial
  Pkwy.
Middlefield, OH 44062
440-834-8888
shooters@shooters-choice.com

Sinclair International
2330 Wayne Haven Street
Fort Wayne, IN 46803
260-493-1858
www.sinclairintl.com

Slip 2000
Superior Products
355 Mandela Pkwy.
Oakland, CA 94607
707-585-8329
www.slip2000.com

Sports Care Products
P.O. Box 589
Aurora, OH 44202
1-888-428-8840

TDP Industries
606 Airport Road
Doylestown, PA 18901
215-345-8687

Tetra Gun Care
FTI, Inc.
8 Vreeland Road
Florham Park, NJ 07932
973-443-0004

Thunder Products
P.O. Box H
San Jose, CA 95151
408-270-4200

Battenfeld Technologies
(Tipton, Frankford Arsenal,
Fajen, Miles Gilbert,
Adams & Bennett)
5885 West Van Horn Tavern
Road
Columbia, MO 65203
1-877-509-9160
www.battenfeldtechnologies.com

White Lightning
Leisure Innovations
1545 Fifth Industrial Court
Bay Shore, NY 11706
1-800-390-9222

RELOADING EQUIPMENT

Ballistic Products, Inc.
P.O. Box 293
Hamel, Minnesota 55340
763-494-9237
www.ballisticproducts.com

Battenfeld Technologies
5885 West Van Horn Tavern
Road
Columbia, MO 65203
1-877-509-9160
www.battenfeldtechnologies.com

Brownells, Inc.
200 South Front Street
Montezuma, IA 50171
641-623-5401
www.brownells.com

Dillon Precision
8009 E. Dillon's Way
Scottsdale, AZ 85260
602-948-8009
www.dillonprecision.com

Hornady
Box 1848
Grand Island, NE 68802
308-382-1390

Lee Precision
4275 Highway U
Hartford, WI 53027
262-673-3075

Lyman Products
475 Smith Street
Middletown, CT 06457
860-632-2020
www.lymanproducts.com

MEC
Mayfield Engineering
715 South Street
Mayville, WI 53050
920-387-4500
www.mecreloaders.com

Ponsness/Warren
768 Ohio Street
Rathdrum, ID 83858
208-687-2231
bsteele@reloaders.com

Precision Reloading
P.O. Box 122
Stafford Springs, CT
  06076–0122
860-684-5680
www.precisionreloading.com

RCBS
P.O. Box 39
Onalaska, WI 54650
1-800-635-7656
www.outers-guncare.com

Spolar Power Load
2273 S. Vista B-2
Bloomington, CA 92316
1-800-227-9667
www.spolargold.com

POWDERS AND COMPONENTS

Accurate Arms
5891 Highway 230 West
McEwen, TN 37101
1-800-416-3006
www.accuratepowder.com

ADCO/NobelSport
4 Draper Street
Woburn, MA 01801
781-935-1799
www.adcosales.com

Alaskan Cartridge
RR2 Box 192F
Hastings, NE 68901–9408
402-463-3415

Alliant Powder Company
P.O. Box 4
State Route 114
Radford, VA 21141–0096
1-800-276-9337
dick-quesenberry@atk.com

Ball Powder Propellant
St. Marks Powder
P.O. Box 222
St. Marks, FL 32355
850-577-2273
srfaintich@stm.gd-ots.com

Ballistic Products, Inc.
P.O. Box 293
Hamel, MN 55340
763-494-9237
www.ballisticproducts.com

Barnes Bullets, Inc.
750 North 2600 West
Lindon, UT 84042
801-756-4222
www.barnesbullets.com

Claybuster Wads
C & D Special Products
309 Sequoya Drive
Hopkinsville, KY 42240
502-885-8088
dmac@spis.net

Clean Shot Technologies
21218 St. Andrews Blvd. #504
Boca Raton, FL 33433
1-888-419-2073
cleanshot@aol.com

Duster Wads
Micro Technologies
1405 Laukant Street
Reedsburg, WI 53959
1-888-438-7837

Hodgdon Powder
6231 Robinson
Shawnee Mission, KS 66201
913-362-9455
info@hodgdon.com

IMR Powder
6733 Mississauga Road
Suite 306
Mississauga, Ontario L5N 6J5
Canada
520-393-1600
www.imrpowder.com

Lawrence Brand Shot
Metalico-Granite City
1200 16th Street
Granite City, IL 62040
618-451-4400

Lee Precision
4275 Highway U
Hartford, WI 53027
262-673-3075

Lightfield Ammunition
P.O. Box 162
Adelphia, NJ 07710
732-462-9200
www.lightfield-ammo.com

Lyman Products
475 Smith Street
Middletown, CT 06457
860-632-2020
www.lymanproducts.com

Polywad
P.O. Box 7916
Macon, GA 31209
1-800-998-0669
www.polywad.com

Reloading Specialties
52901 265th Avenue
Pine Island, MN 55963
507-356-8500

Vihtavuori/Lapua
Kalton-Pettibone
1241 Ellis Street
Bensenville, IL 60106
1-800-683-0464
jbolda@kaltron.com

RamShot Powders
Western Powders
P.O. Box 158
Yellowstone Hill
Miles City, MT 59301
1-800-497-1007
powder@midrivers.com

Sabot Technologies, Inc.
P.O. Box 189
Alum Bank, PA 15521–0189
1-877-704-4868
www.sabottechnologies.com
www.shotgunslugs.com

OTHER CONTACTS

American Gunsmithing
 Institute
1325 Imola Avenue, W. 504
Napa, CA 94559
707-253-0462
www.americangunsmith.com

Second Skin Camo
3434 Buck Mt. Road
Roanoke, VA 24014
540-774-9248
www.trebark.com

SCOPES AND SIGHTS

ADCO Sales
4 Draper Street
Woburn, MA 01801
1-800-775-3687
www.adcosales.com

Aimpoint
7702 Leesburg Pike
Falls Church, VA 22043
1-877-246-7646
www.aimpoint.com

AO Sight Systems
XS Sight Systems
2401 Ludelle Street
Fort Worth, TX 76105

1-888-744-4880
www.xssights.com

BSA Sport
3911 SW 47th Avenue
Suite 914
Ft. Lauderdale, FL 33314
954-581-2144
www.bsaoptics.com

Burris Company
331 East 8th Street
Greeley, CO 80631–9559
970-356-1670
www.burrisoptics.com

Bushnell Performance Optics
(also Tasco)
9200 Cody
Overland Park, KS 66214
1-800-423-3537
www.bushnell.com
www.tasco.com

Deutsche Optik
P.O. Box 601114
San Diego, CA 92160–1114
1-800-225-9407
www.deutscheoptik.com

Fujinon, Inc.
10 High Point Drive
Wayne, NJ 07470
973-633-5600
www.fujinon.jp.co

HiViz Shooting Systems
1841 Heath Parkway
Suite 1
Fort Collins, CO 80524
1-800-589-4315
www.hivizsights.com

Hunter Wicked Optics
3300 W. 71st Avenue
Westminster, CO 80030–
5303

1-800-676-4868
www.huntercompany.com

Ironsighter Company
P.O. Box 85070
Westland, MI 48185
734-326-8731
www.ironsighter.com

Leatherwood/Hi-Lux Optics
2535 West 237th Street
Suite 106
Torrance, CA 90505
310-257-8142
www.leatherwoodoptics.com

Legacy Sports International
(Nikko-Stirling scopes)
206 South Union Street
Alexandria, VA 22314
703-548-4837
www.legacysports.com

Leupold & Stevens
14400 Northwest Greenbriar
Parkway
Beaverton, OR 97006
503-646-9171
www.leupold.com

Millett Sights
16131-K Gothard Street
Huntington Beach, CA
 92647
714-842-5575
www.millettsights.com

Nikon Sport Optics
1300 Walt Whitman Road
Melville, NY 11747
631-547-4200
www.nikonusa.com

Pentax USA
35 Inverness Drive East
Englewood, CO 80112
1-800-877-0155
www.pentaxlightseeker.com

Redfield Optics
ATK
900 Ehlen Drive
Anoka, MN 55303
1-800-322-2342
www.redfieldoptics.com

Schmidt & Bender
Am Grossacker 42
Biebertal

Hessen, Germany 35444
011-49-6409-8115-0
www.schmidt-bender.de

Shepherd Enterprises
2920 North 240th Street
Waterloo, NE 68069
www.shepherdscopes.com

Sightron, Inc.
100 Jeffrey Way
Suite A
Youngsville, NC 27596
919-562-3000
www.sightron.com

Simmons Optics
ATK
900 Ehlen Drive
Anoka, MN 55303
1-800-322-2342
www.simmonsoptics.com

Swarovski Optik
 North America
2 Slater Road
Cranston, RI 02920
401-734-1800
www.swarovskioptik.com

Swift Instruments
952 Dorchester Avenue
Boston, MA 02125
617-436-2960
www.swift-optics.com

Thompson Center
  Company
P.O. Box 5002
Rochester, NH 03867
603-332-2394
www.tcarms.com

Trijicon, Inc.
49385 Shafer Avenue
Wixom, MI 48393
1-800-338-0563
www.trijicon.com

Tru-Glo, Inc.
13745 Neutron Road
Dallas, TX 75244
972-774-0300
www.truglo.com

U.S. Optics Technologies
5900 Dale Street
Buena Park, CA 90621

714-994-4901
www.usoptics.com

Ultra Dot
6304 Riverside Drive
Yankeetown, FL 34498–
  0362
352-447-2255
www.ultradotusa.com

Weaver Optics
ATK
900 Ehlen Drive
Anoka, MN 55303
1-800-322-2342
www.weaveroptics.com

Williams Gun Sight
7389 Lapeer Road
Davison, MI 48423
1-800-530-9028
www.williamsgunsight.com

Carl Zeiss Optics
13005 North Kingston
  Avenue
Chester, VA 23836
1-800-441-3005
www.zeiss.com

MOUNTS AND RINGS

Aimtech Mount Systems
P.O. Box 223
Thomasville, GA 31799–
0223
www.aimtech-mounts.com

B-Square
P.O. Box 11281
Fort Worth, TX 76110-0281
1-800-433-2909
www.b-square.com

Burris Company
331 East 8th Street
Greeley, CO 80631–9559
970-356-1670
www.burrisoptics.com

Custom Quality Mounts
345 West Girard Street
Madison Heights, MI 48071
248-585-1616

Kwik-Site Company
5555 Treadwell
Wayne, MI 48184
734-326-1500
www.kwiksitecorp.com

Leupold & Stevens
14400 Northwest Greenbriar
Parkway
Beaverton, OR 97006
503-646-9171
www.leupold.com

Millett Sights
16131-K Gothard Street
Huntington Beach, CA
92647
714-842-5575
www.millettsights.com

Redfield Mounts
P.O. Box 39
Onalaska, WI 54650
608-781-5800
www.redfield-mounts.com

Simmons Mounts
P.O. Box 39
Onalaska, WI 54650
608-781-5800
www.simmons-mounts.com

Stoney Point Products
1822 North Minnesota Street
New Ulm, MN 56073–0234

507-354-3360
www.stoneypoint.com

Talley Manufacturing
P.O. Box 821
Glenrock, WY 82637
307-436-8724
www.talleyrings.com

Warne Scope Mounts
9057 Southeast Jannsen Road
Clackamas, OR 97015
503-657-5590
www.warnescopemounts.com

Weaver Mounts
P.O. Box 39
Onalaska, WI 54650
608-781-5800
www.weaver-mounts.com

Wideview Scope Mounts
13535 South Highway 16
Rapid City, SD 57702
605-341-3220

INDEX

Camouflage patterns, 166
Camouflaging, 166
Carbon fouling
  cleaning, 203–204
Card-shooting, 80
Care products
  suppliers listed
    website and phone number, 224–228
Case hardening, 190–191
Cast
  definition, 133
Cast adjustment
  pattern board, 137
Cast-off, 133
Cast-on, 133
Ceramic stones, 42
Chamber(s)
  hand-ream, 90
  length, 81
  measuring, 84
  lengthening process, 91–94
Chamber and forcing-cone reamers, 51
Charcoal blueing, 189
Checkering, 122–125
  paper patterns, 124
  shotgun stock
    jig, 123
    styles, 123
    tools required, 124
Checkering kits, 123
Cheek-eez pad
  photo, 155
Cheek-eez
  stick-on adjustment pad, 162
Chemical etching, 89
Choke, 99–110
  constrictions, 56
    bore size, 100
  determining
    drop-in gauge, 106
  dove shooters, 102
  effective range, 105
  efficiency
    determining, 143
  expansion
    T-handled reamer, 108
  ideal range, 105
  shot dispersion, 101
  size
    determining, 101
  sleeves, 104
  steps for installing, 108–110
  systems, 103–105
    adjustable, 104
    Mossberg 835 Ultri-Mag, 105
  tubes, 110
    cleaning, 200

ported, 81
  suppliers listed, 221–223
  vs. wad, 103
Chokes, Briley, 3
Chrome-lining
  barrel, 88
Circassian walnut, 111
Cleaning
  bore
    motorized power scrubber, 198
  frequency, 194
  importance of, 193–205
  purpose, 194–195
Cleaning agents
  photo, 195
Cleaning products
  suppliers listed
    website and phone number, 224–228
Cleaning rods
  manufacturers, 196
  storage
    photo, 22
Cleanliness, 25
Clevis pin, 38
Clymer Manufacturing
  barrel modifications, 106
Cold-blue process, 188–189
Collimator, 181
Colonial Arms
  barrel modifications, 106
ColorWorks
  camouflage, 166
Comb
  adjustment
    pattern board, 137
    measuring drop, 131–132
    vs. pull, 131
  and recoil, 154
Comparison devices, 49
Compartmentalized storage cabinets, 18
Computers, 24
Constriction, 101
Conventional constriction
  bore size, 100
Cotter pin, 38
Coughlin, Jerry, 190
Countertop
  workbench surface, 17
Countertops
  woven fiber mats, 17
Cradle
  cleaning, 199–200
Crosshairs
  alignment, 181
  centering, 179

Refinishing, 121–122
Reloading components
  suppliers, 208
  suppliers listed
    website and phone number, 229–231
Reloading equipment
  suppliers listed
    website and phone number, 228–229
Rem-Choke systems, 104
Remington
  tool layout, 57
Remington 870
  photo, 59
Remington 1100, 64
  photo, 64
Remington Model 11, 64
Remington Models 31 and 870, 60
Remington SP-10
  10 gauge, 57
Replacement stocks
  photo, 112
Report
  loudness, 88–89
Rhino Chokes, 170
Rhino Choke Tubes, 3
Rifled-barrel shotgun, 67
Rifled choke tube
  slug guns, 159
Rifle scope
  mounted on shotguns, 175
Ring adjustments, 180
Ring alignment system
  scope mounting, 178
Rings
  scopes, 178
  screw tightening rotations, 180
Robar's NP3, 190
Rods
  cleaning
    Bore Tech, 196
    manufacturers, 196
    material, 196
    storage, 22
Roll crimp
  slug loads, 211
Roll pin, 37
Roll pin punch, 37
Roper, Sylvester, 99
Roster, Tom, 3
Rotary tools, 30
Round or half-round rasp, 41
Rubber pads
  workbench surface, 17
Ruger Gold Label, 70
Ruger rings, 178
Rule, 49
Rust-blue method, 187–188

S
Sabot fouling
  removal, 196
Sabot slugs
  slug guns, 159
Saddle-style, strap-over scope mount, 173
Safety, 25
  firearms handling
    guidelines, 9
  first-aid kit, 24
  gunsmithing, 8
Salt solution
  quality *vs.* temperature, 188
Savage
  bolt-action shotguns, 67
Savage 210
  photo, 67
Savage Model 720, 64
Saw files, 40
Schultz, Steve, 3
Scooped, 43
Scope(s)
  adjusting, 181–183
  alignment kit, 177–178
  bases, 178
  focusing, 182
  mount
    saddle-style, strap-over, 173
    thread size, 47
  mounting, 173–183
    Brownells ring alignment system, 178
    Da-Mar Gunsmithing, 174
    process, 176–181
    ring alignment system, 178
    rings, 178
    screw tightening rotations, 180
    shotgun, 174–175
    suppliers listed
      website and phone number, 232–233
    zeroing, 182–183
Scoring, 86
Screwdriver
  cost, 34
  quality, 33, 34
Screwdrivers, 31–34
Screw holder gizzie, 51
  photo, 52
Screw-in choke systems
  installing, 105
Screw-in choke tubes, 104
  cleaning, 200
  lubrication, 110
  photo, 104
Screws on sights, 47
  thread size, 47
Sear-notches, 42